SOUL OF THE SKY

Paul M. Breeden

SOUL OF THE SKY

Exploring the Human Side of Weather

Diane Ackerman · Catherine Buni · David Clark · Jan DeBlieu
Jerry Dennis · Annie Dillard · Gretel Ehrlich · Bob Henson
Sebastian Junger · David Laskin · John Mitchell · Chet Raymo
and other authors

———

Compiled and Edited by Dave Thurlow and C. Ralph Adler
Illustrations by Paul M. Breeden

THE MOUNT WASHINGTON OBSERVATORY

A publication of
The Mount Washington Observatory
P.O. Box 2310, North Conway, New Hampshire 03860-2310
www.mountwashington.org

ACKNOWLEDGEMENTS

The editors wish to thank Jeanne Twehous for her editorial assistance, Maureen Rupprecht and Nancy Clark of The Glen Group for their guidance during the early stages of *Soul of the Sky,* and RMC Research Corporation for its in-kind contribution of editorial support. Thanks also to everyone who, in a variety of ways, lent advice, assistance or support to the project; including Peter Crane, Neera Harmon, Chris Costello, Susan Ross-Parent, Bryan Sejvar, Guy Gosselin, Robert Henson, Mary McCusker, Karen Stancik, Judy Thurlow, Bryan Yeaton, Dodie Coman, Bruce Kennett, and Doug Mayer. And most of all, thanks to the contributing authors for their appreciation of weather.

ISBN 0-931134-99-4

First Edition • July 1999

Design and typography by Bruce Kennett Studio
Printed and bound in the U.S.A. by Thomson-Shore, Inc.

CONTENTS

Heard on more than 250 public and commercial radio stations nationwide each day, *The Weather Notebook* offers a two-minute, light-hearted look at weather fact and folklore. *The Weather Notebook* explains weather events and processes in terms that are easy to understand . . . taking the listener on a tour of the inside of a tornado, the architecture of a snowflake, or the weather in your own backyard. Like *Soul of the Sky*, *The Weather Notebook* explores the human side of weather.

Dave Thurlow, host and executive producer of *The Weather Notebook*, as well as writers and correspondents from around the country, bring together their knowledge of weather and the natural world, in an easy-going style. Trained as a meteorologist, Dave has spent many years working in the field of environmental education. A former naturalist and sanctuary manager for the Massachusetts Audubon Society, Dave has led countless field trips in New Hampshire's White Mountains for the Appalachian Mountain Club and was a weather observer at the South Pole.

Jay Allison, winner of the prestigious Edward R. Murrow and Peabody Awards for excellence in radio production, is the show's Senior Series Editor. Bryan Sejvar is the Producer and Sean Doucette the Engineer. Dave Thurlow and Robert Henson are the show's chief writers.

The Weather Notebook is an educational outreach component of The Mount Washington Observatory, and is funded by the National Science Foundation and is underwritten by Subaru of America.

The Mount Washington Observatory

New Hampshire's Mount Washington Observatory, which opened December 1, 1870, was the world's first well-equipped mountaintop observatory. For 22 years, the Observatory (as part of the Army Signal Corps) collected weather data for the National Weather Service. Closed in 1892, the Observatory was reopened in 1932 by private individuals inspired by the majesty of weather at what is known as the site of the "World's Worst Weather." The Observatory uses year-round tours of the station, a summit museum, and educational outreach programs such as *The Weather Notebook* to educate, inspire, and create understanding of the interrelationships of weather and our world. The Observatory's newest initiative, America's first science discovery center devoted entirely to the topic of weather, opened in 1999 in North Conway, N.H.

National Science Foundation

The National Science Foundation (NSF) is an independent U.S. government agency responsible for promoting science engineering, mathematics, and technology through some 20,000 research and education projects annually. NSF provides major funding for *The Weather Notebook* and a portion of its grant to the Mount Washington Observatory has supported the development of this book.

National Oceanic and Atmospheric Administration

The National Oceanic and Atmospheric Administration (NOAA) provides major support for the Mount Washington Observatory and its education programs. NOAA is a major contributor to the development and operation of The Weather Discovery Center, an interactive science center devoted entirely to weather, located in North Conway, New Hampshire.

INTRODUCTION

Take a breath.

Go ahead... a really deep one...

You just inhaled about a tenth of a pound of weather. Well, a tenth of a pound of at-mosphere, actually. A concoction made mostly of nitrogen, oxygen, carbon dioxide and water vapor that surrounds the Earth like a bubble. The bottom few miles of the atmosphere is where weather happens. There it's a living, breathing organism, at times peaceful, angry, generous, unforgiving. And you just drew a part of that in-side you. On average, you'll do that about 12 times or so in the next 60 seconds.

Now, take a look at what you're wearing today. Is it a sweater day? Did you dress in extra layers with a raincoat to top it all off? Or did you opt for a T-shirt and shorts? Your fashion choice was heavily influenced by what the atmosphere was doing over your head this morning.

And how are you feeling? Pretty good about life? Is there a little spring in your step? Or do you feel, as they say, a little under the weather? Your mood has a lot to do with today's sky. A stubborn layer of stratocumulus clouds may have blocked your view of the sun for days, or maybe this is the fifth day in a row of high humid-ity and you wonder when you'll get your next deep, clean breath.

We literally breathe the weather. It affects what we wear, what we eat, how we feel, where we live, how we spend our time. The weather is a major character in the drama of our culture. Imagine reading a history of mankind from a meteorological perspective. Was it a sultry day when Antony first wooed Cleopatra? Did the rhythm of rain drops on a dreary afternoon inspire Cole Porter to write "Anything Goes"? Did the movement of birds and clouds coincide with the image of a flying machine taking shape in DaVinci's mind? Did a winter storm rattle the window in Bob Dylan's room when "Blowin' in the Wind" first popped up on his guitar?

We can guess, with some confidence, that the weather played some part on those landmark days and millions of others in human history. And we can explain the weather mechanics that can lead to moments of terror, appreciation, or epiphany. What we need are stories that somehow bring the two together. That's the reason behind this book.

Soul of the Sky features essays by writers who have looked deeper into how the weather has changed their lives and the lives of others around them. This is writing that inspires, by writers who love to look both inward and outward to observe and ask questions ... questions about ourselves, and questions about the world we live in. Most of the essays are newly written for this book. The rest represent writing that we've encountered and enjoyed over time, essays whose insight and craft have stayed with us.

Among the weather that lies ahead for you in *Soul of the Sky*...

... a lake squall challenges a young boy's feelings about a place he loves

... a pair of tornadoes echo through a town for generations

... a flood unites a community in their sense of belonging to each other

... a puddle returns an adult to her childhood

... a fog bank turns a kayaker's gaze deeply inward

... a "storm of the century" inspires two writers to new career heights

... a thunderstorm shakes a woman's sense of motherhood

... an ice storm redefines what it means to be "civilized"

... a changeable Mount Washington day connects a father and son

... a lightning strike changes almost everything a woman knows about her life

And that's not the half of it! *Soul of the Sky* is a different kind of weather book. Not one preoccupied with charting fronts, defining what an isobar is, or trying to get you to memorize the conversion formula from degrees Centigrade to degrees Fahrenheit, but a collection that illustrates how the weather can inspire, terrify, connect us, and urge us on to new adventures and invite us to gain a deeper understanding of the science of weather and climate.

People often say the one truth about weather is you can't do anything about it. But let's look at another truth. There are two things everyone *can* do about the weather: observe it and understand it a little better every day. These essays help us to see that thinking and feeling are both critical prerequisites to understanding ourselves and our world and one cannot effectively do one without the other.

Try to pick up a few new ideas about the weather from this book. In its own way, each essay in this book is about an adventure – an adventure in understanding the powerful link between our environment and our hearts, a journey of discovery about how the weather shapes and, in many ways, nourishes our humanity.

So take another deep breath and join in these reflections and adventures. Then, next time you're outside, stop, look up for a little while longer than you usually do, and open yourself to the possibility of wonder and understanding there. The sky will do the rest.

Dave Thurlow   *C. Ralph Adler*

This book is dedicated to

Alex McKenzie

SOUL OF THE SKY

LAKE SQUALL, 1967

Jerry Dennis

THE WORLD IS THERE to be seen in its entirety – the whole, astonishing, complex wonder of it at once – but we catch glimpses only. It is our curse. We are not equipped to see the whole picture or to understand it if we could. That is why storms excite us – they force a larger awareness. We're not accustomed to having sudden, massive perceptions thrust upon us. It makes a big impression. We never forget.

When I was a kid I sensed this truth. I was a dreamer, impatient with my limitations and eager for adventure. My family and I lived on a lake a few miles inland from Lake Michigan, and any ordinary day offered opportunities for adventure. But ordinary days bored me. I longed for hailstorms and strong winds, for uncommon weather. When rain chased resorters inside their cabins I took the rowboat out on Long Lake or pestered my parents into driving us to Lake Michigan. I watched the sky for waterspouts and thunderheads. I wanted a life filled with drama. And then one day I learned about drama.

The year I turned 13 salmon returned for the first time to the Platte River and Lake Michigan was alive again. The salmon had been imported as eggs from the Pacific Northwest, raised to smelts in a hatchery on the Platte River, and released with the hope that they could adapt to a freshwater environment in desperate need of help. The Great Lakes had once been among the most productive freshwater fisheries in the world, famous for whitefish, lake trout, perch, and walleye. But early in the century the doors to disaster opened when canals and locks made it possible for invaders to come up the St. Lawrence from the Atlantic, get around the barrier at Niagara, and enter the lakes. The most destructive of the invaders was the sea lamprey, a foot-long, eel-like predator that attaches to fish and sucks their body juices until they die. It took only a few decades for the lamprey to decimate the lakes.

By the 1960s most of the trout and whitefish were gone and 90 percent of the biomass of the Great Lakes was made up of alewives, a small baitfish that invaded the lakes with the lamprey. Alewives reproduce prodigiously, out-competing native species for food and periodically dying by the millions, washing to shore, and fouling beaches. The alewives were an ecological disaster but a potentially rich source of food for salmon and trout. When biologists discovered selective poisons that could control the lamprey population the way was clear for the introduction of coho salmon from the Pacific coast.

The salmon thrived. Their new environment offered outrageously abundant forage, plenty of space, and little competition. They grew to maturity at an unprecedented rate and in August of 1967 began staging off Lake Michigan river mouths in numbers no one could have anticipated. People scouting the lake from aircraft saw schools of salmon three and four miles long swimming toward Platte Bay. The word spread.

A kind of gold-rush mentality prevailed. Anglers drove straight through from Pennsylvania and Tennessee and North Dakota. Most had no idea how to fish for salmon. Many had never visited the Great Lakes and were surprised to learn that it was not possible to see from one shore to the other. Towing the same small boats they used back home for bass and panfish they got in line at the access ramps at the mouth of the Platte River – the queue of vehicles stretching as far as three miles up the road – and when their turn came, backed rapidly down the ramp, hit the brakes, and catapulted their boats into the river. Often in their frenzy to fish they parked their cars and trailers in loose sand beside the road, burying them to the axles, and abandoned them. At midnight they would still be there, digging with their hands and jamming scraps of plywood and carpet under the tires. But that was later. Now they ran to their boats, yanked the starter cords, and were planing at top speed when they reached the gravel shoal where the river met the open lake.

Out in the bay, boats trolled back and forth in confused clots. As many as 1,500 vessels converged on the waters off the Platte. Every type of boat could be seen, from 14-foot runabouts to 40-foot yachts, from 12-foot prams to 30-foot sailboats. My father and I watched in amazement as a fisherman, five miles from shore, paddled past in an aluminum canoe. Once we saw two men crammed inside an eight-foot dinghy that looked more like a bathtub than a boat. It was common to see six adults crowded in a tiny boat with four inches of freeboard.

When the water was calm any boat could handle the lake and any angler who figured out a way to drag a bright lure through the water could catch salmon. The fish averaged 10 to 15 pounds each and were as bright as silver ingots. And like precious metals they inspired a lust for acquisition. People became greedy. They went out in the morning, caught a limit of two salmon per angler, motored to shore to put the fish on ice, then returned to the lake and caught another limit. It was terrific fun. A carnival atmosphere. Now and then tempers flared when someone tried to go out of turn at the access site or if fishing lines from two or three boats got tangled in the water, but spirits ran high and people laughed and shook their heads in wonder at the bizarre things that happened. Salmon "porpoised" from the water, leaping so high they sometimes landed in the laps of surprised anglers. You would troll through a school and everyone would hook a fish at the same time. Sometimes, while you brought one salmon to the net, two or three others would follow and slash at the bright lure in its mouth.

No one had seen anything like it. This lovely vast lake, blue and limpid and bordered by rolling dunes, had been depleted of gamefish for so long that few anglers even considered fishing there. It was a stinking mess in the summer when the alewives died and a scenic desert the rest of the year.

But now the lake produced unbelievable bounty. The local economy boomed overnight. You couldn't find a vacant cabin or motel room in three counties. Every store was cleaned out of its entire stock of fishing lures. Line, sinkers, landing nets, coolers – all were sold out. It was a happy, manic, innocent time.

We had coho fever like everyone else. Saturday and Sunday mornings my father, mother, brother, and I trailered our boat to the mouth of the Platte and got in line at the access ramps. Our runabout was only a 14-footer but it was deep-hulled and more seaworthy than most, with an outboard motor powerful enough to pull a skier and a small trolling motor for back-up. Usually we were on the lake before dawn, our rods set and lures in the water when the sky grew bright.

For weeks the wind was light, the sky clear, the days warm and pleasant. It was easy to believe that it would stay like that forever. But my parents were concerned.

They knew the lake was capable of sudden changes. Mark Dilts, a columnist for the Traverse City *Record-Eagle,* shared their concern. He wrote on September 2: "When the big lake is calm you can paddle around in it in a washtub without any difficulty. But when she begins to kick up her heels she can be a holy terror, making brave men pray for their deliverance from her clutches. . . . Lake Michigan, like a beautiful lady, commands respect from all who know her. For those who have yet to learn this, the lesson can be a costly one. It can even be fatal."

Meteorologists sometimes describe the Great Lakes as weather factories. The five lakes are so large and contain such a tremendous volume of water – about 20 percent of the fresh water on the surface of the planet – that they modify the climate of a significant portion of North America. They extended 575 miles from the northernmost point of Lake Superior to the southernmost point of Lake Erie, a latitudinal difference of eight degrees. From west to east they stretch more than 800 miles, about the distance from Chicago to Dallas. Their surface area of 95,000 square miles is greater than the combined areas of New York, New Jersey, Connecticut, Massachusetts, Vermont, New Hampshire, and Rhode Island.

Equally significant is the geographic location of the lakes. They straddle the 45th parallel, halfway between the North Pole and the equator. Like all mid-latitude regions of the earth, the sun's angle of inclination and the length of the days varies greatly as the seasons progress, making winters cold and summers relatively warm. Furthermore, the lakes are located near the center of a vast, wedge-shaped trough cutting north and south across the middle of the continent. This lowland trough allows cold, dry air from the Canadian north and warm, moisture-laden air from the Gulf of Mexico to flow relatively unhindered toward one another. With no mountain ranges to block their passage, the air masses come and go, driven by the wave-like undulations of the jet stream, producing hot weather when the jet stream loops north and cold weather when it loops south.

All these factors contribute to make the Great Lakes an extraordinarily active weather zone. Locals are justified in saying that if you don't like the weather, wait five minutes. Temperatures can swing 40 degrees in a few hours. Cold fronts sweep down from the north with almost no warning, driving warm, humid air upward, forming clouds and precipitation. Violent weather often results.

Autumn is an especially unstable season around the Great Lakes. The surface water is often warmer than the air, so as cool wind from the land passes over the lakes it picks up heat and moisture. The warming air becomes more buoyant and rises, carrying moisture with it and creating turbulent winds and isolated storms. Larger systems of storms surging east across the Great Plains encounter the lakes and intensify. By the time they cross to the far shores they can be monsters.

That Saturday of the autumn equinox, September 23, 1967, promised to be another fine day. Friday's forecast gave no indication of trouble: "Saturday partly cloudy and a little warmer, with a chance of showers near evening. Northerly winds . . . light and variable." For weeks newspapers across the country had published newswire reports raving about the spectacular fishing in Platte Bay. Thousands of anglers finished work Friday, loaded their boats, and drove north to go fishing.

But early Saturday morning the weather took an unexpected turn. A shift in the jet stream brought a cold front down from Canada. At 4:30, when the alarm went off, we could hear the wind in the trees. My mother argued for staying at home. Dad and I talked her into giving it a try.

At dawn we stood beside the tiny weather station near the mouth of the river. A single red pennant snapped in the wind above us. Small-craft warnings. The phrase had potency, if you knew the Great Lakes. My father had spent enough time on them to be wary. My mother was even more cautious. She had grown up on the shore of Lake Michigan a few miles north of Platte Bay, and had spent her childhood walking the beaches and listening to stories of storms and shipwrecks told by her father, who had been a Coast Guard life-saver at the station in Glen Haven. All of us had seen storms from shore, had watched gigantic waves batter breakwalls and lighthouses and send spray surging 20 feet in the air. The shoals around the Manitou and Fox islands had wrecked dozens of ships. Sometimes after storms we found artifacts on the beach – the ancient ribs and keels of sailing ships, each a reminder of the lake's power and our frailty. I had been out with my father in three-foot waves so choppy they seemed about to break our boat to pieces. Even much larger craft were at risk when the waves exceeded four or five feet. Some sailors said the Great Lakes could be more dangerous than the Atlantic. The waves were not the regular swells of an ocean. They were tight and steep and unpredictable. They could break a boat in half.

To the west the sky was dark with squall lines. Already the lake was the color of steel and booming with whitecaps. During the drive to the Platte, while it was still dark, we had listened to weather reports announcing waves two to three feet high and winds of 25 knots. It was hard to ignore the warnings.

Many anglers ignored them nonetheless. Those who had driven long distances were especially reluctant to stay on shore. After traveling all night to reach the lake they refused to be stopped by a few waves. Besides, others were going out, hundreds of them, and there was comfort in numbers. The general assumption was that small-craft warnings were a formality, a way the Coast Guard and the National Weather Service could avoid liability should someone run into trouble. Ignore them and the waves might go down. One thing was certain: you couldn't catch anything on shore.

So they went out. The Coast Guard estimated that more than a thousand boats motored into the waves beneath that moiling black sky. My father and I watched them. We stood on shore with the wind in our faces, smelling the big-water smell of the lake and the stench of the salmon guts spilling from garbage cans in the parking lot. We watched anglers one after another launch their boats and motor down the estuary at the end of the river until they met the breakers at the mouth. Their bows rose toward the sky and fell, like military tanks busting over berms. The waves struck the boats and sent up spouts of spray that were quickly sheared off and blown like smoke toward shore. A few boats turned back at the mouth and retreated upriver, their passengers shaking their heads in defeat. But for every one that returned there were six or eight waiting to challenge the waves.

All morning conditions worsened. By afternoon the wind had reached 40 miles per hour and the waves were six to eight feet high. The air was filled with the roar of wind. Yet hundreds of anglers stayed on the lake and fished. Not until boats began to swamp in the waves did they take the storm seriously.

At first they tried to reach safety by maneuvering through the ranks of breakers at the mouth of the river. The only way past the gravel bar was through a single narrow channel where the strongest current flowed. It was tricky, even in calm water. In the high waves, boats came in from all directions and wedged in the channel. They rammed one another, turned sideways in the current, swamped when waves broke over them. Soon dozens of boats were engulfed.

More timid boaters stood offshore, hoping the wind would change and the seas diminish. They circled out there, fighting the waves until their fear of the open lake overwhelmed their fear of the breakers and they made a dash toward the beach, adjusting their throttles to the waves in an effort to run aground between them. They came in, their engines laboring one moment and screaming the next as the water fell beneath them, and six or eight of us would run down with the descending wash and grab the boats by their gunwales and bow lines. The men inside jumped out to help and the women and children crouched against the decks with terrible looks on their faces, and we would pull the boats as far up the streaming slope of the beach as we could before they were slammed by incoming waves. We were successful only with small boats. Larger ones were too heavy to pull. We would hold them as best as we could while they wallowed in the surge until the next wave washed over their sterns, dumping a roiling froth of water and sand inside. A few waves later the boats would be awash in the surf or anchored to the bottom with sand.

Rumors ran up and down the beach. Hundreds missing, presumed dead. Dozens of bodies washed up at Frankfort. Dead children at Empire. Boats sinking far out in the bay, beyond help.

It would be days before we learned that seven men died. The dozens reported missing would all be accounted for. Everyone would say it was a wonder more didn't die. Coast Guard helicopters lowered baskets to floundering anglers and lifted six of them to safety. Two men clung to the side of their capsized boat for more than two hours until, exhausted from the waves and the 50-degree water, they lost consciousness. Somehow people on shore waded through the surf and dragged them to safety. One rescuer said that of the 15 or 20 boats he helped drag onto the beach at Empire, only two contained life preservers.

My father and I helped as much as we could. Dad had been a police officer and was trained to save lives. I knew he could rescue anyone in danger. The knowledge was exhilarating. It made me more competent just to be with him. I felt capable of adult heroics.

Late in the afternoon we watched a small boat with two men inside circle beyond the breakers. They seemed unsure of themselves. They had seen others try without success to run the gauntlet of crashing waves and were looking for a way to save their boat. They circled, rising on each wave, disappearing into each trough, their heads swiveling as their boat turned, always facing shore. You could see them working up their courage. Finally they steered toward the beach. Instead of accelerating like the others, they came slowly, their engine at trolling speed. They went up on a wave, down in a trough, up on another wave. Once they went down in a trough and did not come up. When the wave passed the men were in the water.

They were not far from shore. We could see the hair plastered to their heads, could see the expressions on their faces. They looked more surprised than frightened. Their eyes were big and they worked their mouths, as if apologizing. They would bob in the water in their orange life preservers until a wave came over them, then they would disappear in the froth.

Waves broke with so much force the ground shuddered. I stood on the beach above the reach of the water and felt the dull impact through my feet. My tennis shoes were soaked and full of sand and my socks had fallen down around my heels. I thought it remarkable that I could feel those tons of falling water through the earth.

The breakers shoved the men toward shore, then dragged them away, but allowed them to get no closer. A current pulled them down the beach away from us. We walked beside them, shielding our eyes from the spray and sand thrown at us by the wind. Every wave broke over the men and made them tumble in the foam. They turned upside down and kicked their legs as if trying to run. The wave would pass and they would struggle in the trough, splashing with their arms. The life jackets seemed to inhibit more than help them.

People on shore ran down to the water's edge carrying coils of rope and tried to throw them. The ropes would unfurl and hang for a moment in the wind, then come back. One man knotted a rope around his waist and waded into the waves but he was knocked down, and others pulled him back against his will. Waves broke one after another over the men and they disappeared each time in the froth, with only a glimpse of orange showing.

A woman standing near us held her hands to her face and screamed for somebody to do something.

I had sand in my eyes. I turned away and rubbed them and turned back and saw the faces of the men. I made eye contact with one of them. He was overweight and gray, the age of my grandfather. He could have been our insurance man or the guy who delivered bottled gas. He seemed apologetic. Every time a wave pounded him he came up looking a little more apologetic. He seemed to try to smile at me.

Children were excused from responsibility, but I was no longer a child. I was old enough to help. I pitched on a baseball team and could have thrown a rope better than anyone. I could have heaved it low and hard beneath the wind and made it straighten like a bullwhip and land within reach of first one man, then the other. I was lean and fast and swam well. I could have tied a line around my waist and dived through each wave the moment before it broke and reached the men in the calm of a trough and spoken reassuring words to them as the people on shore pulled us to safety.

A wave broke over them. Their legs rose in the air but did not kick. Another wave came and objects slick and dark rolled heavily in the spume, like logs. My father gripped me high on my arm and turned me away. I tried to look back but he gripped harder and pulled. An ambulance waited in the parking lot, its lights flashing urgently. People ran, shouting, their voices torn to fragments by the wind.

The men in the water wore bright orange life preservers with bulky collars that supported their heads above the water. They should have been safe. Everyone said if you wore a life preserver you were safe. The Coast Guard guaranteed it. Our parents said so.

I had wanted to be a hero. I had longed for drama in my life.

My father gripped my arm and pulled me across the parking lot past the ambulance, past people holding their hands over their faces. He put me in the car with my brother and my mother. They had been there all along, watching. I will never forget the looks on their faces.

For weeks I lay in bed at night hearing the roar of the storm and feeling the awful draining power of the waves. I wanted to remain a child, but it was too late. Childhood fades with the knowledge of peril, and peril is everywhere. My father could not protect me from it. No life preserver could save me.

They died a hundred feet from shore.

Jerry Dennis writes for such publications as Smithsonian, Sports Afield, Wildlife Conservation, Gray's Sporting Journal, *and* The New York Times. *His latest book is* The River Home *(St. Martin's Press) and his previous books,* It's Raining Frogs and Fishes *and* A Place on the Water, *have been widely praised and have been translated into four languages. He lives in Traverse City, Michigan.*

*"One must have a mind of winter
To regard the frost and the boughs
Of the pine-trees crusted with snow..."*
– WALLACE STEVENS, *"THE SNOW MAN"*

A MIND OF WINTER
[A WRITER'S QUEST]

David Laskin

THERE WAS JUST ONE WEEK TO GO until spring and the sun shone brightly over New York City. The air temperature had been rising steadily through the morning, and by midday it hovered in the low 40s. Manhattan office workers on their lunch breaks were walking around with their coats unbuttoned and smiles on their faces, at least some of their faces. Not a lick of wind to cut the sunshine. March 12, 1993. Friday. You could practically taste the weekend.

I heard the blizzard warning early that afternoon while I was browsing in a Fifth Avenue bookstore (they still *had* bookstores on Fifth Avenue back then). A clerk at the cash register had a radio on. The music stopped and those scary, end-of-the-world bleeps came over the air: "This is not a test. Repeat. This is not a test." *The voice of doom.* "This is a broadcast of the Emergency Broadcast System. A blizzard warning has been issued for Saturday for the New York City metropolitan area, Long Island, New Jersey, and Connecticut. Repeat: A blizzard warning ..." Gritting my teeth a little, I paid for my books and headed back out into the sunshine. Not a cloud in the sky. Maybe a faint smudge of gray over the Hudson. Blizzard? Nah. No way. Never happen.

Sixteen hours later, when I woke up in my house near the north shore of Long Island, two to three inches of fresh snow covered the earth and more was coming down fast. An occasional gust of wind eddied the flakes. My kids were jumping for joy. So they nailed it after all, I was thinking, as I flipped from channel to channel on television. It was all snow all the time on the major networks, with hyperbole piling up faster than drifts. "Armageddon!" a reporter hollered on CNN. "The mother of all blizzards!" I felt my scalp begin to tingle with excitement. What a stroke of luck. I had recently embarked on the daunting project of writing a history of weather in the United States, and here I was in the thick of it – history, *history*, roaring up the East Coast and into my back yard. Now it was my duty as a weather historian to hang tough at my command post by the television, wasn't it?

Around the time of the tenth cut "back to Gene at the Channel 3 Weather Center," I snapped out of the vacuum tube trance and went out in it. The storm was strangely serene after the relentless hysteria of the airwaves. Absence hit me first – absence of traffic noise, absence of color, absence of business as usual. The air was thick and muffled in steadily falling snow. The wind biting but not punishing. Not yet anyway. By the time I got to our local park fronting west on Long Island Sound, the gusts were picking up. I could see maybe twenty yards out into the water, which looked dark and menacing in a world gone white. Beautiful, but also terrible. Sensation in my toes was starting to go and an icy trickle dripped down my spine.

Just how foolhardy was this little walk of mine? I'd read enough stories of pioneers freezing to death in blizzards only steps away from their warm sodhouses; of violent cold fronts plunging temperatures so fast that wet travelers became encased in literal coats of ice; of frigid wind blowing hard enough to suck the air out of people's mouths and suffocate them. Six-and-a-half years before I'd stood at my living room window and watched, jaw agape, as ten seconds of hurricane Gloria's wind snapped half the trees in my backyard – trees that were 70, 80 years old, reduced to firewood in a couple of heartbeats. *What if it doesn't stop?* I thought at the time. *What if it just keeps on blowing until the windows break and the roof blows off? What's to stop it?* And now an even bigger weather event – the Storm of the Century – was loose upon the world and here I was standing out of doors, alone, a couple of miles from my house, with nothing between me and the elements but mittens and a ski parka. Hadn't the National Weather Service issued those warnings? Hadn't they predicted that this was going to be like a combination of blizzard *and* hurricane? Hadn't everything they said come uncannily true so far? Was I nuts?

Nuts and lucky. As it turned out, I made it home without incident, a tad disappointed that I hadn't racked up more of an adventure. After all, this was a "Storm of Historic Proportions," as the television weather folks kept crowing, and all I had to show for it was numb toes and a sore back from helping push a Mercedes out of a snowdrift. Where was the history? As far as I was concerned, this was just an old-fashioned snow storm, the kind that used to make me jump for joy when I was a kid.

It wasn't until the next day, when I read about the extent of the storm in the newspaper and the damage it inflicted on life and property from Alabama to Maine, that I understood what I, along with one third of the other people in the United States, had lived through: At least 219 deaths from Cuba to Canada (later estimates ran as high as 272 – more than three times as many people as hurricanes Hugo and Andrew killed together). Property damage estimated at over $2 billion. Fifty inches of snow on Mount Mitchell, North Carolina; 47 inches in Grantsville, Maryland; 43 in Syracuse, New York; 13 in Birmingham, Alabama. Record low pressure in Worcester, Massachusetts, Washington, D.C., Richmond, Virginia, Raleigh, North Carolina. Three million people without electricity. More than fifty tornadoes in Florida's panhandle and a nine-to-twelve-foot storm surge along Florida's Gulf Coast. Winds of 135 miles per hour reported on New Hampshire's Mount Washington. For the first time ever, a single storm shut down every major airport on the East Coast. Altogether, meteorologists estimated, some 44 million acre-feet of water (one acre-foot is the amount of water that would stand one foot deep over one acre of land) had fallen during the storm – more water than flows out of the mouth of the Mississippi River in forty days.

But in the drumroll of awesome statistics, there was something missing. The Storm of the Century was historic not only for the extent of the damage it inflicted, but also for the accuracy of the forecast that heralded it. And, in a strange way, the forecast was the only aspect of the storm I had *really* experienced: the most furious winds steered clear of my corner of Long Island, the deepest drifts piled up elsewhere, the center of the low skirted around us, we even managed to avoid the communal discomfort of power outages. But I had heard those other-worldly blizzard warnings on that sunny Friday afternoon; and it was that forecast, that immaculately, preternaturally accurate forecast as it turned out to be, that hummed in the back of my mind as I waded out into the silent snowbound streets.

How did they know?

In turning this storm into history, I saw the forecast as an element just as crucial as the destruction of life and property. Destruction – lives lost, dollars blown – is the crude anthropomorphic grid we fit over a storm to measure its impact on society. But isn't the forecast a far more refined and complicated way of assessing the reality of a storm? Science applied to nature; reason against chaos; brainpower versus atmospheric power. The weather forecast and all the technology and expertise and passion that went into it was the only human endeavor that came anywhere near the intensity and magnificence of the storm itself. Certainly the talking heads on TV didn't touch it; nor did my solitary stroll; nor did the chilling statistics I read in the paper the next morning, though the statistics at least provided one wide-ranging objective measure. It dawned on me that if I wanted to comprehend and convey the history of this cataclysm we had just lived through, I needed to talk to the people who had generated this forecast. They were the critical link between the storm and our experience of it.

Two months later I was doing 30 on the Capital Beltway, pushing my Toyota through one of those heavy, muggy, white-shirt-wilting heat waves that Washington D.C. is famous for. Only mid-May and the Storm of the Century was already a distant memory as far as the atmosphere was concerned, the foot-and-a-half of snow that had piled up on the Maryland and Virginia landscape gone without a trace, absorbed into the earth and sucked back up into the weepy tidewater humidity. It was high noon and sultry as hell as I exited the Beltway at Camp Springs, Maryland and merged into the flow of traffic on a four-lane suburban boulevard. My destination was the headquarters of the National Meteorological Center (subsequently renamed and reorganized as the National Center for Environmental Prediction) and according to the crystal-clear directions I'd taken the trouble of printing off my computer in bold face — `a quarter mile off the Beltway, NMC is on the left, parking lot behind it` — it should have been right in front of me. But I still drove by the building twice before I convinced myself to turn in and park. How could this drab, nondescript, dentist-office kind of place be the national center of *anything*? Where were the marble columns? the uniformed guards? the eagles clutching lightning bolts? The only clue that something special happens here was an inconspicuous sign over the entrance: World Weather Building. And yet, as I was about to learn, despite the absence of visible symbols, this building is as critical to our nation's weather as the Pentagon is to our defense. For the NMC is the innermost nerve bundle of the central nervous system of the National Weather Service. The NMC is where national weather comes into focus. All the maps you see in newspapers, all those cold fronts and low-pressure systems your television weathercaster grins over, all those long-range outlooks they flash up on the Weather Channel: they all originate here. This is where the global data networks converge; this is where the megacomputers re run; this is where the nation's weather happens: the NMC is Weather Central.

It was here, on the computer terminals of what was then called the Meteorological Operations Division (MOD), that the Storm of the Century began.

Five days before the "event," before a wisp of cloud or a lick of wind, before so much as a smudge appeared on radar screens, MOD chief Dr. Louis Uccellini (who has since moved on to become director of the Office of Meteorology) and his NMC staffers were already aware that something very strange and very powerful was brewing. As luck would have it, Lou Uccellini was my first interview of the day and he was the perfect guide to the Storm of the Century. Tall and gangling of build, intense of manner, quick of wit, short of temper, blessed with a Long Island accent you could measure on the Richter scale, funded with an immense store of knowledge and enthusiasm for weather, especially winter weather, and an equal supply of patience for those who know less than he does (most especially me), Lou Uccellini literally wrote the book on whopper snow storms – *Snowstorms Along the Northeast Coast of the United States, 1955–1985*, co-authored with Paul Kocin. Here was the living, breathing embodiment of that bull's-eye Storm of the Century forecast. If anyone was going to connect me to this facet of weather history, here was the man.

It turned out to be one of the most rewarding interviews I've ever conducted. Not only did Uccellini bring passion and expertise to the subject, he was desperate to make me understand what he was talking about. Understand is too weak a verb. I had to *get it*. The deeper and wider he perceived my ignorance to be (I am a free-lance writer with a great love of weather but not a lick of science) the farther back he went in his explanation. I had to know about how computer forecast models work – how meteorologists make discrete the "continuous fluid" of the atmosphere into measurable chunks known as grid points and assign each of those points a value based on atmospheric readings; I had to understand how a monster supercomputer known as the Cray YMP-832, housed in climate controlled splendor in nearby Suitland, Maryland, ingests the current atmospheric readings (temperature, humidity, air pressure) and then, using a different set of equations for each model, calculates how these readings will affect the weather in ten minutes, and then in ten minutes after that, and so on, in ten-minute increments out to forty-eight hours or, during one run each day, out to ten days; I had to see that even minuscule variations in the initial data fed into Cray can result in tremendous differences in the ultimate forecast. Or rather, not forecast but "guidance," for Cray does not spit out "cloudy, rain developing overnight" or "two feet of snow by sundown," only people do that after studying the texts, maps, charts and graphics that Cray routinely produces as part of the "national guidance package." Basically, what Lou Uccellini gave me in the course of two hours was a crash course in contemporary meteorology. For which I have been boundlessly grateful ever since.

"Nothing was there on Monday," Uccellini noted, handing me maps and charts showing the range of barometric pressures predicted by five different models. Each new chart jumped half a day closer to the storm. I could see that the millibar numbers were all over the place. With each jump, the models kept changing their "minds" about the intensity of the low and the path it was likely to take – one predicting rain, another placing the storm track well inland. But there was one exception to the vacillation: the NMC's Medium-Range Forecast (MRF) model. In run after computer run, the MRF model was consistent. Uccellini fanned the documents out so I could see what he was talking about: "The MRF model kept showing that a complex interaction of features was blowing up in the Gulf of Mexico. This was our signal that a major storm was coming, that a powerful low was going to form over southeast Georgia on Saturday morning, and we chose to believe it and stick to our guns. The consistency of the MRF model locked us into the forecast."

By Tuesday night, March 9, Uccellini's team of meteorologists became convinced that this was not going to be just another howling winter storm, but would be a "major precipitation event" depositing its heaviest snow over western Virginia. By Wednesday night, March 10, they were mapping out significant snowfall from Alabama to Maine. Three days before the storm hit, the NMC issued the first predictions for ten inches of snow along the coast, with two to three *feet* inland. And now the phrase "historic proportions" began to appear in NMC communiqués. "This was unprecedented," Uccellini confided proudly, getting swept up once again in the drama of the storm. "A few years back we would never have predicted more than four inches this far in advance. With this storm we had unprecedented lead time based on forecast models. We had unprecedented accord with local offices, and unprecedented effort to get the media plugged in to alert the public." By dawn on Friday, the ordinarily terse, colorless Weather Forecast Branch bulletins were screaming like tabloid headlines: "A great storm is approaching ... monster low [moving] up the East Coast ..." "One of the great winter storms in Eastern U.S. History ..."

And yet, Uccellini admitted that when people from the media swarmed into the NMC on Friday for a briefing, he was "sweating bullets" of anxiety that his office might have overhyped the storm. "CBS wanted me to call it the Storm of the Century, and in fact the phrase has been attributed to me," he told me. "But I refused to do it. The century's not over yet."

In any case, whoever coined it, the Storm of the Century is the title that stuck and nobody so far as I know has contested it.

"What would have happened if the storm had fizzled?" I couldn't resist asking Uccellini.

"I admit I was a nervous wreck Friday night," he replied. "If it had turned to rain at Pittsburgh, it could have been the bust of the century. If this forecast was wrong, after all the hype, we would have gone out the window. Literally. It would have set us back ten years in credibility." But of course they didn't have to worry about that. It turned out to be a hell of a forecast for a hell of a storm.

Once the NMC decided to place all its chips on the epic snow accumulations indicated by the MRF model, it was up to meteorologists at the local National Weather Service forecast offices up and down the East Coast to refine the NMC "guidance package" and apply it to local conditions. The "zone forecasts," as these county- or city-wide near-term forecasts are called, make up a mosaic of Little Pictures within the Big Picture painted by the NMC. So, in the New York City metropolitan area, the zone forecast called for more snow accumulating in the higher elevations of New Jersey and in upper Westchester County and advised that the snow might mix with or briefly turn to rain along the coastal sections, which was in fact what happened. "We have a multitude of microclimates in this region," one lead forecaster at a NWS forecast office told me, "and we can take these local conditions into account in a way that the national guidance package can't." The forecast offices covering the major East Coast cities began issuing winter storm watches on Thursday, at which point the media siege commenced. Emergency managers went into high gear. On Friday, the decision was made to activate the Emergency Broadcast System and issue the blizzard warnings that I heard in that Fifth Avenue bookstore.

Ironically, it was at this point, the eleventh hour, the point of no return, that confidence in the forecast began to totter among those in the know. The models were beginning to wobble a bit and some private forecasting companies bailed out, backing off the heavy snow forecast or calling for rain. But the NWS stuck to its guns: it was really too late to put them down.

By Saturday morning, NWS staffers, much to their professional relief, were snowbound, along with the rest of us, in the storm they had known about all week. And the rest, as they say, is history.

The heat wave broke the evening before I was due to leave Washington. A vigorous squall line pushed through from the west, kicking up gusty winds and dumping down over an inch of rain in half an hour. A Maryland woman died when a tree fell on her car. Awesome, uncontrollable, the weather never stops making history.

Only now, after the better part of a week immersed in the inner workings of the National Weather Service, it was a history I felt I had some connection to. Weather doesn't just happen – it happens to us. Around us *and* inside us. It's something we experience individually and collectively, through our senses and through the latest computer, satellite and radar technology. The MRF model and the icy trickle down my back, the lives lost in storms and the lives saved due to timely storm warnings, the television hype and the emotion recollected in tranquillity: at the intersection of all these elements, *that's* where I was going to find the history of this incredible storm. Not man against nature: man *in* nature – with science as the window and the grid and the screen and the shield between them.

As I drove back north up Interstate 95 the next day under fair skies and clean westerly winds, I felt the history of this event begin to crystallize in my mind like a fluent, finished globe. Thanks to Lou Uccellini and other members of the NWS, I had a handle on one of the great winter storms of recent times – a handle that took me far beyond what I had experienced myself or seen on television or pieced together from talking to friends and neighbors. The globe began to revolve in my mind. How strange that I had actually lived through the storm and walked as far as I dared into the teeth of it, and yet only now, driving home at the end of a late spring heat wave after hours of conversation in drab government offices, did I feel I knew anything real about it. But that's how history is made, or least my history of the Storm of the Century.

So there it was, a chapter of my book spinning before my eyes. Now all I had to do was go home and get it down on paper.

David Laskin, a Seattle-based freelance writer and lifelong weather enthusiast, is the author of two recent histories of weather in the United States – Braving The Elements: The Stormy History of American Weather *(Anchor Books/Doubleday) and* Rains All The Time: A Connoisseur's History of Weather in the Pacific Northwest *(Sasquatch). Laskin's articles about weather, travel, gardening, parenting, and American literature have appeared in a number of national publications, including* The New York Times, The Washington Post, Smithsonian Magazine, Parents Magazine, *and* Travel & Leisure. *Laskin keeps an eye on the weather in company with his wife and their three daughters from their North Seattle home.*

AN INTERVIEW WITH
Sebastian Junger

This article is excerpted from an interview
conducted for *The Weather Notebook* radio program
by Andrew Morrell at New Hampshire Public Radio.

How did you come by your interest in weather?
I've grown up by the sea. I grew up outside Boston and lived in Gloucester, I lived on
Cape Cod. The weather is more dramatic at sea. You can go down to the beach and
see there's an interaction between air and water that is much more violent than the

interaction between ground and air. Water and air really interact in savage ways. As a writer, and as a person, it's a more compelling place to be. And, like the desert, you have this tremendous sweep of horizon, you can see three or four different kinds of weather happening at the same time in different parts of the sky. You see the complexity of the atmosphere, the complexity of the world, in a place like that.

I was in Gloucester when this storm [described in *A Perfect Storm*] hit. I saw 30-foot waves crashing against the coast, destroying houses, and that was a tremendously moving experience. In New England, weather is very much a part of your life and some of my most intense memories and feelings from childhood are associated with really clean, clear fall days or a really sultry summer. The weather is part of my emotional life. It's impossible for me to smell woodsmoke on a clear, sharp day and not think of being a child in New England in the fall.

I remember I was working overseas, in a war actually, as a journalist. It was summer and it was starting to get cold and I stepped on a dead leaf on the pavement in Zagra, Croatia. It was a dead oak leaf and just the sound of that crackling made me instantly homesick. In a way, that's my most intense weather experience.

We had a blizzard in 1978 that has been likened to the storm I wrote about. I think we had three feet of snow in Boston. It paralyzed Boston, people were stuck on Route 128. I was 16, 17 years old and I couldn't go to school for a week. It was fantastic to see society paralyzed. It was so gratifying that we don't control everything. I just loved that. I was walking around in the woods at night, watching the snow come down. It wasn't even that cold. It was just absolute ecstasy that something this wild could happen right on the edge of a major city. That just absolutely thrilled me and I thought, God, I wish we had a storm like this every month.

I know most people think bad weather is a pain in the neck, and it can be. But if you really stop to think about it, you're witnessing something much more dramatic than anything you can see on a movie screen. One thunderstorm is the most dramatic thing people will see, and they don't even know it.

You seem to like life "on the edge." Why?
Well, the edge is where things happen. You can go to human history and see where cultures clash ... of course, that's where wars are but there's also a fertile area of exchange of ideas. And likewise with meteorology. You have warm air and cold air clashing, so you have interesting weather. Same thing with the Gulf Stream hitting the Labrador current. You've got these tremendous banks of fog that roll in and just envelop the Grand Banks, which are the fishing grounds south of Newfoundland. That is a very fertile environment for fish. The swordfish, the big biologic fish, live in warm water and dart across into the cold water to feed on the plankton. But the swordfish don't want to live in cold water so they collect – the whole food chain tends to collect along the boundaries. The fishing boats collect along the temperature breaks because that's where the fish are. These two worlds collide.

People keep asking me, "why do you do things that are dangerous?" It's a bit of a pat answer, but it's true: when you do things that are dangerous, your senses are heightened and you feel more alive. I've never felt more alive than watching that storm hit the coast of Gloucester. I was so wound up by the forces of nature screaming all around me, that I almost could not stand still. I was like a little kid. I mean, if your senses remain at the same level in that situation, you've got a problem.

What aspects of weather do you find most fascinating?
The most basic thing that intrigues me is how wind works. Everyone knows what wind is and no one, me included, ever stops to think about how it works.

Warm air has a lower pressure. There's less air per cubic foot in a warm air mass, and cold air has higher pressure. If you have a mass of warm air next to a mass of cold air, as you know, nature hates a vacuum. The cold air rushes in to fill the sort of "barometric hole" that's next to it in the warm air. It's just nature, trying to even things out. So when you feel wind, it's just cold air rushing in to fill a sort of hole in the atmosphere. So if you have a cold front near a hurricane, which is very warm air, the winds will be particularly strong, the hole is that much deeper. Now every time I feel the wind I think, "Oh, okay, cold air rushing toward warm air." That's all it is.

What was so unique about the Storm of the Century?
It was meteorologically perfect. A National Weather Service meteorologist I interviewed said that so many variables had to line up to produce a storm that lasted four days, that retrograded back toward the coast. That means it went against the typical path of the jetstream and hit the East coast a second time and produced waves that were over 100 feet. Typically, all weather goes east to west with the flow of the jetstream. This storm passed off shore, then it stopped and merged with Hurricane Grace, and turned around and came back. It caused billions of dollars worth of damage to the coast and produced these huge, huge seas that ultimately sank a swordfishing boat.

There was a storm in 1898 called the Portland Gale that they think did something similar ... a nor'easter that merged with a hurricane. So that was almost 100 years before, coincidentally, so it's not a common thing at all.

Where were you during the storm?
I was living in Gloucester. I was writing, in my apartment, when I noticed right before the storm hit (I didn't know it was coming) this strange moaning sound coming from the telephone lines. I had never heard this before. I ran outside and realized it was the wind moving through the phone lines at speeds that I had never experienced before. The sound was just unearthly, this sort of moaning scream. Apparently that's very well known on fishing boats as the wind moves through the rigging and the outrigger cables, producing some ungodly sounds. It was described as a really

deep kind of tonal vibration that sounded like a church organ, played by a child. A church organ played by a child is one of the creepiest images I can think of, offhand. A child is sort of capricious, and that's exactly what the weather is, in a way.

Every single person [in A Perfect Storm] is united through this storm. Not through the Coast Guard, not through premonitions, not through New England, not through fishing. I saw the storm as almost a murderer who is careering around the country killing people. They're united by this one force that no one can control. Some people were dragged into the storm and disappeared and some people were dragged in and spat back out alive. I started the book with what people were doing a month before the storm hit and ended it with how the storm affected these people's lives two years later. The last ripple effects didn't dissipate for years and I was intrigued by that – how profoundly a storm like that can affect people and ripple through their lives for years and even generations. I mean, there are children who lost fathers whose lives will be dominated by that fact; you could trace the effect of this storm several generations. That fascinates me.

Why are storms like this one so powerful over the ocean?
The air over ocean water soaks up a lot of moisture and hurricanes start when warm air becomes saturated with moisture. The moisture precipitates out as the air rises and it sets up convection cells, which start to spin and eventually you have a hurricane. Over the North Atlantic, you have subtropical air clashing with colder air from Canada. The clash of temperatures and air densities makes for a very volatile system. Moisture allows a storm to grow stronger, it's a kind of fuel.

A storm over the water, even over the Great Lakes, produces huge waves. The same storm over land, the storm I wrote about, would have been completely unnoticed. The wind speeds were not particularly strong, even though they blew for four days. But the land doesn't move. Sometimes trees will snap, but that's about it. Over water, waves driven by the wind just get bigger and bigger. After four days, you have 100-foot wave heights.

A confused sea is when the waves are coming from many different directions. If there are swells that are 40, 50 feet high, they're not breaking, a boat can ride them out fairly well. They all come from one direction, the sea has a chance to sort them out, they become more orderly, more even. But the closer you get to the storm, the sea can come from almost any direction. There is no way to keep the bow of the ship into the oncoming seas, which is the safest position to be in. Suddenly you can get a sea on your stern or off your portside, or on your starboard side, and you can be rolled over. It's absolutely chaotic and very, very hard to survive.

What is life like for men who work on the sea?
I used a quote from Heart of Darkness in my book describing an expedition that goes into the jungle and Conrad says that "the jungle closed in behind the expedition like

the sea closing in over a diver." Then word came back weeks later that all the donkeys were dead, and I thought that was a perfect description of what happens to people who go to sea and then all you get back is a little bit of wreckage.

I've never been to sea, I've never worked as a fisherman, but the people I've talked to who have been out in storms tell me that the ocean in a storm is an incredible, alien, harsh environment ... you think it's like being on Mars. You think human beings have absolutely no business being in this environment and there is no way I will ever get out of this alive. They look out over the crest of waves, this ravaged ocean, it's stretching from horizon to horizon, and they think "we've got to get through or we're going to die." The overwhelming feeling is we have no business being here and we can't possibly survive it.

When the weather comes in, it completely dominates the sky ... there are no mountain ranges, no trees, nothing between you and it. There's nowhere to hide. That is something fishermen are very aware of, on their own in a small boat. Anything they can see, anything that's on the radar, they have to handle in a 70 foot boat. Of course, it turns them all into amateur meteorologists because they're really interested in this thing that could kill them at any moment.

I think people at sea continue to die in ways that people haven't even thought of yet. The machinery on boats is dangerous. Guys can get dragged overboard by the hook, get impaled by the hooks coming on board. A lot of guys die because they get up in the middle of the night to urinate, walk to the back of the boat, and a freak, small little wave pops them overboard. There's a saying, "most guys drown with their flies down" for that reason.

Instead of getting very paranoid [about the weather], fishermen get fatalistic about it. The sense was there are certain waves and certain storms that there is no way to survive, even on a fairly large ship. "If my time's come, my time's come," and that really seems to be how they deal with the danger. One fisherman I talked to had just come in from a trip, he looked out at the water and said, "you know, the ocean, she's beautiful, she's a beautiful woman, but she'll kill you without a second thought." In that sentence you have both his love of the sea and his understanding that tomorrow he could be dead.

I'm a little low to generalize too much about anybody, but by and large, fishermen are a pretty rough crowd. Swordfishermen are off shore for a month at a time. They can make a tremendous amount of money or not any money at all. They're on shore for a week and go out again for a month. You can imagine in their week on shore, the whole month of living that they couldn't do when they're at sea packed into that week. Some guys are married and have mortgages and go home and are with their families. But my feeling is that the only way they can get through a month at sea is to promise themselves a kind of mini-Mardi Gras when they get home. I would do exactly the same thing. That's why I'm not a fisherman. It's a really difficult way to live, it's hell on families and girlfriends and children.

A lot of these guys end up without real homes and families because they can't keep them together.

That said, I should say I started hanging out at the Crow's Nest, which is a bar in Gloucester. The mother of one of the guys who sank in this boat works as a bartender there. I'm not a fisherman, I'm not from Gloucester, so these people had every reason not to talk to me much. They were incredibly friendly and hospitable and welcoming after they sort of checked me out. So in some ways I would say their bark is worse than their bite. They look like some rough characters, but actually they're fantastic people and just have incredible stories to tell.

Sebastian Junger is a freelance journalist who writes for numerous magazines, including Outside, American Heritage, *and* Men's Journal, *where he is a contributing editor. His 1997 non-fiction work,* The Perfect Storm, *is highly acclaimed as one of the greatest books ever dealing with the subject of weather and the sea. He has lived most of his life on the Massachusetts coast and now resides in New York City.*

A Memorable Easter Ice Storm

Mary Reed Long

ILLINOIS HAD ITS WORST WINTER on record in 1977–78, a melancholy distinction brought about by a total of 18 severe storms, the first of which arrived in the closing days of November. The last, and most severe, was saved for the turn of March.

March is a month that traditionally roars in like a lion but goes out like a lamb, but in 1978 it left more like a penguin. In central Illinois we had a veritable smorgasbord of bad weather, with a storm which lasted from the early morning of the 24th to the wee hours of the 26th (followed by 12 more hours of light snow). For most of the storm, precipitation was in the form of freezing rain, but at one time or another, the rain was mixed with ice pellets, drizzle, fog, and even a snowflake or two. It simply could not make up its mind at first, as the temperature hovered around freezing, but in the end it settled for a fair amount of freezing rain, which left central Illinois with up to an inch of ice coating everything outdoors.

We had watched this accumulation, which reminded me of the sugar glaze on doughnuts, all morning. By the afternoon of 24 March, Good Friday, the trees in our garden had a curious appearance. They were encased in ice, with what appeared to be piles of broken glass beneath them, pieces of ice blown from over-weighted branches and shattered on the stone-hard ground. By tea-time the same day, the mesh on our screen-door resembled dappled glass under its coating of frozen rain, an opaque layer which obstructed our view.

By nightfall both front and back doors were frozen shut. We could have opened them with some effort, of course, but, we reasoned, why break the ice-seal, when it kept draughts out? Then, at about ten to ten on the evening of Good Friday, our lights began to flicker, and finally died. We tried several switches, looked in the fuse-box, and then looked outside. We were not alone in the dark, for most of the city was blacked-out, too. Or would be, in a short while, after the spectacular display of natural fireworks which was enlivening the night sky. It was quite a sight, with numerous flaring blue flashes and showers of white sparks as power-lines fell under the weight of accumulated ice and a gusty wind.

Pieces of broken branches littered our street, electricity-meters leaned drunkenly away from walls, and the roadway looked like a black mirror. Peering out of an iced-up window, we could see a thin halo of fuzzy yellow light on the horizon, marking a couple of sub-divisions which, by a quirk of fate (or, more likely, underground cables) kept their electricity through it all. Across the way, someone was out with a flashlight, its beam stabbing up and down, pinpointing fallen power-lines and tipsy-looking poles leaning every which way.

As there wasn't much we could do except make jokes about being powerless in two senses of the word, we turned on the radio, since the TV station had gone. The storm had been responsible for the fall of a couple of TV towers, and more than one radio mast, and other stations could not broadcast (nor be received) for lack of power. One of them later reported that the bulk of those who rang them up to complain to them (or their meteorologist) about the weather were unhappy about missing the basketball games. This was before the callers had fully grasped the impact of the storm; later on they would have a lot more to worry about than basketball games.

In any event, we did find a couple of radio stations which stayed on the air, though at half-power, by ingeniously rigging-up batteries, desperation being the mother of invention. The one we listened to took off its usual programming and opened up the lines for a five-hour "phone-in". Listeners rang up with questions on such diverse topics as how to keep tropical fish alive, or what to do about a furnace which could not be turned off, and then other listeners telephoned offers of help, or advice on the problem. And there were certainly plenty of problems, state-wide. Over a million people were without electricity, and power-crews were out in the bitter cold and a wind cutting to the bone, struggling to restore service. Some crews were to work for 72 hours straight. Many would be brought in from out-of-state to assist, so there were, of course, protests about the cost of it all – after the power was back on, needless to say. Right then, though, they were heroes, laboring under dreadful conditions alleviated somewhat by coffee and food and blankets brought to them by local householders.

And they deserved it all, too. In our city alone, almost all the primary, and almost three-quarters of the secondary, systems were down. It was the beginning of a memorable Easter weekend.

So that Good Friday evening we sat around, wrapped in sleeping-bags, in a candle-lit room, listening to the radio. After an hour or so, public service announcements came through – boil water orders and the like – along with lists of streets and highways closed to traffic. Closure was sometimes due to local police department action, sometimes to accidents. We were fortunate to be at home, for thousands of others had to spend the night (and subsequent nights, in some cases) in motels, truck-stops, school halls and wherever they could find shelter. Some were stranded in cars and trucks, out in the open; a few did not live to tell the tale. Emergency committees were working at full pace, evacuating residents from unheated nursing homes, or finding warm places for elderly people, or the young, in such facilities as had their own generators. All the local hospitals had them, so there was no need to move patients, but a lot of other people were still being evacuated on Easter Sunday.

By early Saturday morning, it was obvious that there would be no power restored that night, so we went to bed.

The following day, things were really organized. Line crews worked on, snatching sleep as they could. City and local taverns were closed by order of the police department, in a measure to prevent disorderliness. Drunk driving was not much of a problem, though, as not only were the taverns closed, but little petrol was available. This was due not only to the difficulty in getting supplies through, but also the fact that most pumps are operated by electricity.

If one had to travel – and repeatedly, strong warnings were broadcast that it was best to stay home – one could try to get to the railway station. Trains were running occasionally, though hours late. They were packed with passengers. The interstate and secondary roads were getting glassier by the moment, if they weren't already closed. The airport was closed, but Greyhound, like doggies, kept on rolling, though very slowly and extremely carefully.

Most people decided to stay home. There were two problems to be faced there: the question of food and of keeping warm. The emergency committees were delivering hot meals (which had to be carried up seemingly-endless flights of stairs in high-rises whose lifts were inoperative) and some shops did well for a time, as in the case of one hamburger parlor which sold five thousand dollars worth of food in a few hours before it lost its electricity and had to close.

Other businesses also flourished, especially those selling items such as blankets, warm clothing, camping stoves and the like. Edibles were a big seller, and in some cases the shelves were cleared, less because of panic-buying (though there was certainly some of that) than the difficulty in getting fresh deliveries. We had a fair amount of food, mostly tinned, since having weathered (no pun intended) one Illinois winter, we had entered our second with a cache of tinned and dried goods, powdered milk, and candles. As it happened, our stove had been repaired two days before Easter, on the same day, in fact, that our refrigerator arrived. Whilst waiting for the latter, we had kept milk between back and screen doors, where bitterly cold air kept it fresh. So much so, in fact, that some mornings we had chunks of frozen milk on our cereal. This reminded me of my first day at school in England, where our one-third-pint bottles of milk were also frozen solid and had to be lined up along the steam-pipes which heated our classroom in order to thaw. (This free milk has since been discontinued, thus giving Prime Minister Mrs. Thatcher the nickname of "Milk Snatcher" in certain of the popular papers in the UK.)

Our newly arrived refrigerator had scarcely reached the cooling point when the electricity went. Thus there was not a lot of food in it, so we did not have the problem which faced owners of well-stocked freezers, to wit, what to do with pounds of food before it spoiled. Some people, such as our next-door neighbors, solved it by taking the entire freezer off to friends who still had power. Others (ironically) found space for their edibles at cold-storage facilities. Yet others cooked the lot and invited friends to share the repast.

We had a small problem in the four pounds or so of bread-dough which I had stored in our 'fridge. By Saturday evening, this was rising at an alarming rate, so, bowing to the inevitable and working by candlelight, I baked for a couple of hours, turning out rolls, loaves, and that great love of the sweet-toothed American, cinnamon rings. We distributed these around the street, and then settled down to another evening of radio; our station was broadcasting items from the "golden years" of radio, I remember – Burns and Allen and so on. However, as the situation in Illinois was receiving attention on the hourly news bulletins, we rang up relatives in North Carolina to assure them that we were coping, and that they were not to worry about us.

They assured us most sincerely that they had not been worrying about us at all, as they had not heard a thing about it until our call. On Saturday evening the Chief of Police broadcast a warning that he had double the usual number of officers out on patrol, and that anyone caught committing burglary would, under the current emergency, automatically be charged with looting. Many of the smaller towns around us were already under curfew, but he did not, he said, intend to declare one for us unless everyone in the city lost their power – and a few kept it. Some of the smaller towns had also lost their telephone services, but contact was maintained with the "outside" by radio hams and by the CB network.

By Sunday, a couple more radio stations were broadcasting again, as was one TV affiliate, or so we heard. We couldn't actually see it, of course. Another station resumed services by borrowing a generator belonging to a local drum and bugle corps, but its output was too weak to reach where we were, which seemed a pity, after going to all that effort.

On Sunday afternoon, a nearby township tried to restore its water by floating a National Guard generator downriver on a flat-bed barge. Unfortunately, its power was not sufficient to run the pumping station, but the attempt was a typical example of good old Yankee ingenuity. And of something else – the excellent spirit and neighborliness displayed all weekend. People really seemed to try to do the best they could to help each other – rallying in the face of a common enemy, perhaps – opening homes to people stranded without heat, checking houses whose owners had had to leave to go to shelters, and sharing food and warm clothing. Apparently this had also struck a local clergyman who broadcast, on Easter Sunday, that people do indeed need people. Even more remarkable was the sense of humor displayed by most under what one could call, at the very least, trying circumstances.

That Easter Sunday afternoon about a dozen of us gathered at a neighbor's house for coffee and conversation, and, later, a pot-luck dinner of huge platters of fried chicken, spaghetti, and rolls. As we were new to the area, it was an excellent opportunity for us to meet our fellow residents, although one could not exactly call it a house-warming. I do not have much luck with house-warmings, anyway. Years before, in an English village, a house-warming that I held was enlivened by the explosion of a neighbor's garage. We summoned the local volunteer fire brigade and then the entire party went around the corner to fight the blaze until they arrived (in seven minutes, an excellent time, we thought.) Thus we got to meet a fair number of the villagers and not just our neighbors.

On Sunday afternoon, then, we sat in the kitchen watching birds scratching for crumbs by the back door. Younger folk played cards in the living room. Us oldsters sat around chatting as the coffee pot perked on the stove. "And so do you have winters like this in England?" I was asked. Even harking back to family legends about the winter of 1947 – when snow was up to the window-sills, there were two babies under three (and two older children) in the house and coal was still on ration – I had to admit that, normally, we did not.

One of the neighbors, who lived in an all-electric house, could not even cook or make tea. We had a gas stove, which proved our salvation, in that hot food and drinks kept us going. Our heating was also gas, which was fine except that the thermostat which controlled it was electric, so there was no heating on at all. (We did not, of course, use the stove as a source of heat, an extremely dangerous practice.) It was, in fact, a couple of days before we discovered that we still had hot water available. In a cold house, with cold water, showers had necessarily been brief, and therefore the water did not run long enough to get to the heated stuff. As we had a gas heater, we can only surmise that the thermostat on it was mechanical and not electrical.

In the meantime we kept warm by hauling dead wood and debris to the curb for later pick-up by the city. While we were at it, we demolished an old wooden fence and an unused dog house in the back garden, things which we had been meaning to do for some time. Our lives were, I thought, a little like those of the pioneers – at least in the hours which we kept. It was early to bed (for candles, even with cunningly-wrought aluminum foil screens around their backs, simply do not provide enough light to read or write by) and early to rise (since one had to keep moving to stay warm).

Easter Monday was sunny, though still bitterly cold. The sun melted off most of the snow and some of the ice, making it possible for people to get further afield and take stock of the damage. It was appalling, but especially so in the older, more heavily-wooded neighborhoods, which were also areas where utilities tended to be carried on above-ground poles. Many of these were down, but even worse were the noble old trees, some planted in the last century, so badly damaged or actually fallen down. Half-stripped of boughs, they leaned all over the place, sometimes blocking the street, or in a few cases toppled on cars. People got to work, dragging and stacking, and huge hedges of branches and such sprouted along the sides of the roads, forming tunnels down which emergency vehicles slid and skated, red lights flashing.

I do not recall seeing one bird's nest on the ground, though I did spot one balancing precariously in a fork just below the point where the branch broke. Evidently birds know their business. Those which had survived the wintery blast (and many did not) were out and about, chirping as loudly as ever. Since there was not much traffic other than the birds, the world seemed eerily quiet. Here and there, as we worked round the garden, we found rabbit-tracks. Rabbits had stripped the bark from some of the bushes, but I didn't begrudge them it. The toll on wildlife must have been extraordinarily high. On Easter Monday, too, it was announced that the Governor had closed all state agencies, to keep roads clear for essential traffic. Most shops and offices followed suit, so people worked at home; many of them would not be able to return to work until the following week. Thus the telephone lines were very busy, as happens after any extraordinary event. If alien invaders ever come, the telephone companies are going to make the biggest profits in their history – at least until their lines are destroyed by laser-gun fire, crashing UFOs, or the advancing artillery with which we traditionally greet such visitors (in films at least).

Out in the country things were even worse than in the city, for farmers had to feed, water and tend to their stock by hand. Work in the fields was, of course, impossible. Stockmen milked cows by hand, but even then, more often than not, the milk simply could not be collected, for even if tankers from the dairy managed to get through, no electricity was available for pumping milk into them. And livestock suffered badly.

On Tuesday evening, we left our street for the first time in five days to go and see friends in a nearby town. Driving along in the dark was very odd, for even on the blackest night, there is always a slight glow along the horizon, a reflection from the lights in town, but that glow was missing on this occasion. Along the way, leaning utility poles and downed lines were abundant, black cables snaking across ditches or draped on fences. Occasionally we passed a farm where a few kerosene lights showed, but mostly it was dark.

Returning to the city about eleven, we saw lights in the distance. Had the power returned? Indeed it had, and it looked as if every light in our street had been turned on, blazing out the message that at about 9:30 P.M. on 28 March, electricity had been restored. Some of the other towns were not so lucky, though, for it took almost a fortnight to get them connected back on to the grid.

A week after the storm, a friend announced her pregnancy, to be greeted with a cry of "first victim of the ice storm!" although apparently there was no significant increase in the local birth-rate in late 1978 or early 1979. Rubbish pickup and mail delivery soon were resumed, rubble was cleared away, and people began to return to work, many of them sporting "I Survived the Ice-Storm of '78" T-shirts. The state, of course, also survived, albeit battered, and life soon got back to normal.

The man on the corner, when the thaw came and the time was right, planted four new trees. All of them continue to flourish.

Mary Reed Long, a columnist for Weatherwise *magazine and an occasional contributor to* The Weather Notebook, *writes about weather, mythology, history, museums, and folk customs. Her Byzantine mystery novel,* One for Sorrow, *(co-authored with Eric Mayer) will be published in the summer of 1999. Her article for* Soul of the Sky *first appeared in the April 1987 issue of* Weatherwise *magazine, and is used by permission of the publisher, Heldref Publications.*

RAGE ON GRASSY RIDGE

Christine Woodside

TO MY LIST OF FEARS – the dark, strange dogs, wasps, and ladders – I added a dread of thunderstorms after the night of April 22, 1997. My two young daughters and I spent that night inside a tent while thunder, winds, and rain whipped across Grassy Ridge, an open saddle at 6,050 feet in the Appalachian Mountains at the Tennessee–North Carolina border.

The gray clouds rolling in that evening did not look threatening. It was not cold when we leftbut the temperature dipped as the storm moved in over our campsite. Long stretches of wind and driving rain hit between about midnight and dawn. I sat up most of the night trying to stop the tent from swaying. I stretched my arms into a beam to hold up the tent while the storm lashed from the northwest at a 45-degree angle against the nylon.

Going into that night, I had slept in a tent in the Appalachian Mountains about 45 times, and in trail-side shelters at least 80 times. I'd never had rain like this. In the spring of 1987, the year I hiked the entire Appalachian Trail, I trudged through daily afternoon thunderstorms for about 10 days. During one deluge, lightning ripped open a tree a quarter mile north of where I stood huddled with my friend, Cay. At the crash of electricity destroying the tree trunk, I practically jumped into her arms in fear. But a moment later, we started hiking again. We saw the giant shards strewn down the forested incline. I wasn't scared, just impressed. I liked thunderstorms. I relished the sweet smell of a downpour that breaks long days of strangling heat.

I had driven more than 800 miles to the grassy highlands of Tennessee and North Carolina from our house in Connecticut to make reality out of an idle dream. "Did you know there are mountains with just grass growing on top?" I asked my daughters Elizabeth and Annie, ages eight and six, one night as I was putting them to bed. One of them said, "I want to see them."

"I'll take you there someday," I promised, the nightlight casting a comfortable shadow on their round cheeks.

When we got to Carver's Gap, the girls galloped away from the car, while I put the last things in my pack. The mountain was just as I'd advertised: a neat mound of grass rising impressively into scuttling light-gray clouds and patches of late-afternoon sun.

We saw three people hiking down towards us as we made our way up Round Bald. The half-hidden sun was at our backs while, at our right, great clouds drifted slowly from south to north.

"Are you camping out?" the grandmotherly woman said, smiling. She and two children were finishing their adventure for the day. Did she think we were imprudent to set out with those clouds rolling in? I was used to walking through all kinds of weather. I did not tell Annie and Elizabeth that the radio announcer had droned on about a "one hundred percent chance of rain tonight and tomorrow." We were still an hour from our mountain when I heard that. Weather is regional, changeable, and forecasts in the East often can't stay ahead of what really happens. I always like to gamble on the optimistic side. The announcer also said nothing about lightning and thunder.

"Yes," I smiled up at the woman. We smirked at one another as mothers do in public. Our expressions said we both knew how hard it is to get children out on a hike. I was weighed down with most of the gear, stuffed into the same sea-green pack I'd been using for 10 years. My girls carried their own clothes in their school packs. They wore whistles on nylon cords around their necks. Each had in her pack a tiny spiral note pad and pencil, on which to draw and write, and a tiny flashlight.

The hike started out straight to the east, beyond a fence and over a stile, going up stone steps through the turf, which still was dead though this was the beginning of spring. Within 15 minutes we were sitting on a large rock eating peanut M&Ms. We continued our gentle climb to the highest part of Round Bald, the first peak, which was not much higher than the road. "Look, girls," I kept saying, admiring the expanse on either side. The grass reached away to air and clouds on all sides.

The trail forked. We could go left to stay on the Appalachian Trail, 1.4 miles more to a three-sided Appalachian Trail shelter, or we could head about a half mile south to a grassy campsite with a spring nearby. My plan was for us to head on the left fork the next day. For tonight, I'd picked the route to the right, which led to the closer campsite with no shelter. My desire was always to stay one step ahead of my children's complaining, to get them to something beautiful in a few miles.

Within a few minutes, without climbing much at all, we were at the highest open peak in the Southern Appalachians (others have trees or buildings on top), a lonely meadow full of alder. I high-stepped through some of this undergrowth to see if it was our campsite, and I found the plaque honoring farmers who used to live there.

It was still partially sunny when the ridge rolled down into a little col. "This is it," I said. The girls came to life, hurling down their packs, and grabbing their notebooks. They perched on a giant rock at the edge of undergrowth of rhododendron. They drew pictures of the grass, the few trees jutting up, the rocks framing distant ridges, and of me, pulling out the gear. I began to taste the fear of full responsibility.

I struggled with the tent. The outer layer, the fly, wasn't quite right. This was a tent I hadn't put up in several years. We had two others we used more often, but this was bigger. I just jammed the metal pins in and the fly was hanging askew but covering the entrance flap. As soon as it was up the girls jumped inside and settled into the sleeping bags.

I reached into the pack for the food bag. The girls were chattering away. I decided to slip away down the eastern slope to fill up the nylon water bag. I didn't tell them where I was going. I found the spring in a tenth of a mile. A PVC pipe neatly routed the water over rocks. I squatted for a few minutes in the dusky light, holding the bag's opening under the pipe. But when I got back to the tent it was raining lightly and the girls were standing outside the tent in their stocking feet.

"What are you doing out in the rain in your socks?" I panted as I lugged the water up to them.

They turned toward my voice, darted toward me and cried out, "Mama!" My heart lurched. I'd scared them by disappearing. "I didn't know if I should blow my whistle," Annie said. Her emergency whistle was in case she was lost. I felt terrible, but hid it beneath a briskness. "OK, well go back inside the tent and I'll have spaghetti ready in a minute." The air was going gray, and misty rain continued to sift downwards.

I pumped the little lever on the gas stove and got it going. The pot boiled, the spaghetti cooked in a lump. I got the pasta mix envelope open and I wrenched open the little can of tomato paste. I mixed it up and took the whole pot in to the girls. I barely had time to be grateful for the hot meal that makes camping sweet when the pouring rain came and then thunder crashed.

"I'm sad," Elizabeth said, with little emotion. It sounded like an announcement. Annie let loose with, "I'm scared, Mama!" She cried as the lightning flashed. I admit, I was really scared. I knew lightning strikes the highest thing. There we were on an open ridge in a tent with metal poles. The guidebooks say tents are as dangerous as convertible cars at a time like this. Still, I comforted myself by recalling the couple of pines near us that were higher up.

Then the lightning and thunder were only about a second apart and I said fast, "Say a prayer." Annie started wailing again. Why did I say that? I thought. Elizabeth sat silent at my left. I reached inward for control.

"Girls, there are two mountains on either side of us. They'll protect us from the lightning. We are going to be OK," I said.

What I didn't say was my fear of what would happen if the lightning happened to be exactly where we were. I felt this sickening panic, an urge to jump out of the tent and start running in any direction. Then I thought of how dark it was now, and I tried to modulate my breathing and remain calm. I'm not usually a calm person in an emergency. When my husband fell against a razor-sharp tree branch and cut open his head on Baldpate Mountain in Maine, it was Cay who bandaged him up while I stood with my back to the scene, muttering, "Oh my God."

Our storm raged for two distinct periods. First the thunder crashed and rain poured straight onto us for about two hours. During this time, I decided we weren't bothering to brush our teeth and we would go to sleep. It was so loud that I yelled the nightly prayer, *"now I lay me down to sleep!"*, and I sang whatever hymn I could remember. Elizabeth hummed with me. I reached into their packs for their raincoats to cover the sleeping bags, in case water dripped in. It was then I realized Annie had no raincoat.

The afternoon in the car came back to me: "Mama, I can't fit my raincoat." "Don't worry, Annie, I'll help you with it when we get to the trail." So I pulled out my waterproof pack cover and put that on top of her. Both of them rolled over and, by some miracle, fell asleep.

I sat up through this first deluge. When it stopped, I peeked outside of the tent flap. Behind the clouds there had to be a moon. Its light filtered through the fog. It was dead quiet. I went outside to relieve myself and I thought how beautiful it was. Still, I was tense. I crawled back inside and lay down, thinking that maybe we'd be dry enough in the morning to continue on three miles northeast to the Overmountain Shelter in the morning. Under a good roof it wouldn't matter how much it rained.

Then came the second hell. I guessed it was about 1 A.M. This time there was no thunder or lightning, but a driving wind and rain. The wind would whistle as the tent walls swayed back and forth and then there'd be these long bursts of loud spattering rain on the fabric. Sitting up between the girls, I felt very lonely. At my left, Elizabeth now was awake, but she didn't say anything. My feet were a little damp, the sleeping bag was heavy with the water it had soaked up, and I kept pulling my girls' limp bodies away from the little rivulets of water at the side.

It was then I knew we weren't going to the Overmountain Shelter in the morning. We were going to march straight back to the car. Suddenly I thought, "How will we see in the fog?" Open ridges are notoriously hard to cross then. Then I recalled the trails through the balds are chiseled deep in the meadow grass. They are actually trenches a few feet deep. We couldn't get lost.

Ages later, the rain lightened up enough that I could tell it was done. I lay down and almost dozed off, until I could tell the sun was up. I crawled outside, glad to be OK, disappointed that my camping trip was disintegrating before my eyes, and worried the stove wouldn't light. But I had kept both the stove and the matches, inside their zip-loc bag, in my pack next to me, and the flame roared. I was not a vigilant cook this morning. The cream of wheat congealed into a giant lump.

They suited up, silently, but I was left to eat most of the cereal, which made me wretch. Then they had to come outside and stand around while I dismantled the sagging tent. My hands seized up as I tried to pull out the pins and stuff the sopping mess of fabric into the sack. Behind me, Annie was standing lost inside my gigantic raincoat. "My hands are cold," she wailed, *"waaaaaaah!"* Elizabeth just stood there.

I marched around jamming stuff into my pack. The frying pan I'd bought at a pharmacy somewhere in Virginia was not going to hold our pancakes and I could not fit it in. I set it by the cooking rock. Annie angrily took off my raincoat, said it was too big, and handed it back to me. I faced my grim charges and announced, "OK, let's go. Just keep walking. You can't stop this morning. You'll get cold. We're going to keep going. You can do it."

"Yeeeeeeeeeuh!" Annie wept as she stepped up out of the col through the mud with her high-top sneakers, pajamas, shorts, and fleece jacket with tiny drops all over its fuzz.

"Let's count the flowers, girls," I said desperately. We were going to start counting the tiny bluets, the wildflowers in the turf, on the way out, and I guessed there would be 10. I was thinking how hikers usually get into trouble just when they think they're out of it. They get hurt going down a mountain, for instance, or they get lost and sometimes die within a mile of civilization.

We counted more than 400 bluets. Annie stopped crying and laughed at me because I'd thought there would only be 10. We even pulled out the instant box camera and snapped shots of each other along the ridge.

Eighteen months after this happened, I set out to document the terrible storm we'd survived. What did I find? This incident, which proved I could not recognize thunderclouds at high elevations and which tested my ability to care for my children, was an ordinary storm.

Even the temperature was not remarkable. It hit the low 40s overnight (about 10 degrees below the usual). The bursts of rain after midnight, which resembled the angry hand of God trying to prove something to me, measured less than an inch.

In Asheville, North Carolina, about 48 miles southwest of our campsite, roughly three-quarters of an inch was recorded on the 22nd, while on the 23rd, a half-inch. In Bristol, Tennessee, about 32 miles north of our tent, a fraction of an inch fell on the 22nd, and between midnight the 23rd and through that next day, only 3/5 of an inch.

A fraction of an inch, taking me to the edge of my courage. There I was in this less-than-an-inch, trying to sing an old Quaker hymn, but only bits of the words would come back to me. "My life goes on in endless song, above Earth's lamentation ... no storm can shake my inmost calm, while to that rock I'm clinging ..." For miles in either direction, there were no humans but us, sometimes forgetting to breathe inside our little swaying tent. It was too dark to see if my daughters were peering at me with trusting eyes or screaming inside with terror. As I did, they pretended they could handle it, and so they could.

Spring in the southern mountains brings wintry cold and tragedy. People expect it. On the 18th, most of western North Carolina seized up under a freeze that damaged apple orchards. The evening before our night on Grassy Ridge, a storm raged in eastern Tennessee and much of North Carolina, leaving giant hailstones, some of them as large as golf balls. Also the night before our experience, a "short line segment convection," a wind formation, roared east-northeast from Georgia to South Carolina, knocking over trees and power lines and damaging 46 buildings.

The afternoon after our trial, a red oak tree in central Tennessee was struck by lightning, and weather observers said chunks of wood 75 pounds apiece flew 50 yards through the air, a piece of tree got embedded in the taillight of a car, and the lightning dug a trench almost three feet deep along the tree root system as it tunneled toward a house.

Considering those storms that we missed, my timing was great. I picked one night in the high country that brought a typical storm. Only my fingers were numb. There were no snowdrifts or piles of ice. The tent stayed up. I remembered to take the stove inside before the rain started, and my children were stoic. We had luck and grit. Still this night will remain a mystery to me. It was worse than the records from nearby towns could reflect. I will never know how fast the wind was hurtling into my tent as I braced my left arm against it. They don't have a weather station at 6,050 feet.

This was a ridge where scientists could not measure a storm by what it knocked down: there were no buildings, people, no power lines, no mobile homes to cave in, and no large trees. There were just the ancient rhododendron near clumps of pines and our tent with me inside forming a human beam with my arms. Inside, I suffered the uprooting of my security. That can't be rebuilt.

Christine Woodside is the environmental writer for The Day, *a daily newspaper in New London, Connecticut. She lives in Deep River, a small town on the Connecticut River, with her husband and two daughters, ages eight and ten. She hiked the entire Appalachian Trail in 1987.*

FLOOD

Annie Dillard

IT'S SUMMER. We had some deep spring sunshine about a month ago, in a drought; the nights were cold. It's been gray sporadically, but not oppressively, and rainy for a week, and I would think: When is the real hot stuff coming, the mind-melting weeding weather? It was rainy again this morning, the same spring rain, and then this afternoon a different rain came: a pounding, three-minute shower. And when it was over, the cloud dissolved to haze. I can't see Tinker Mountain. It's summer now: the heat is on. It's summer now all summer long.

The season changed two hours ago. Will my life change as well? This is a time for resolutions, revolutions. The animals are going wild. I must have seen ten rabbits in as many minutes. Baltimore orioles are here; brown thrashers seem to be nesting down by Tinker Creek across the road. The coot is still around, big as a Thanksgiving turkey, and as careless; it doesn't even glance at a barking dog.

The creek's up. When the rain stopped today I walked across the road to the downed log by the steer crossing. The steers were across the creek, a black clot on a distant hill. High water had touched my log, the log I sit on, and dumped a smooth slope of muck in its lee. The water itself was an opaque pale green, like pulverized jade, still high and very fast, lightless, like no earthly water. A dog I've never seen before, thin as death, was flushing rabbits.

A knot of yellow, fleshy somethings had grown up by the log. They didn't seem to have either proper stems or proper flowers, but instead only blind, featureless growth, like etiolated potato sprouts in a root cellar. I tried to dig one up from the crumbly soil, but they all apparently grew from a single, well-rooted corm, so I let them go.

Still, the day had an air of menace. A broken whiskey bottle by the log, the brown tip of a snake's tail disappearing between two rocks on the hill at my back, the rabbit the dog nearly caught, the rabies I knew was in the county, the bees who kept unaccountably fumbling at my forehead with their furred feet . . .

I headed over to the new woods by the creek, the motorbike woods. They were strangely empty. The air was so steamy I could barely see. The ravine separating the woods from the field had filled during high water, and a dead tan mud clogged it now. The horny orange roots of one tree on the ravine's jagged bank had been stripped of soil; now the roots hung, an empty net in the air, clutching an incongruous light bulb stranded by receding waters. For the entire time that I walked in the woods, four jays flew around me very slowly, acting generally odd, and screaming on two held notes. There wasn't a breath of wind.

Coming out of the woods, I heard loud shots; they reverberated ominously in the damp air. But when I walked up the road, I saw what it was, and the dread quality of the whole afternoon vanished at once. It was a couple of garbage trucks, huge trash compacters humped like armadillos, and they were making their engines backfire to impress my neighbors' pretty daughters, high school girls who had just been let off the school bus. The long-haired girls strayed into giggling clumps at the corner of the road; the garbage trucks sped away gloriously, as if they had been the Tarleton twins on thoroughbreds cantering away from the gates of Tara. In the distance a white vapor was rising from the waters of Carvin's Cove and catching in trailing tufts in the mountains' sides. I stood on my own porch, exhilarated, unwilling to go indoors.

* * *

It was just this time last year that we had the flood. It was Hurricane Agnes, really, but by the time it got here, the weather bureau had demoted it to a tropical storm. I see by a clipping I saved that the date was June twenty-first, the solstice, midsummer's night, the longest daylight of the year; but I didn't notice it at the time. Everything was so exciting, and so very dark.

All it did was rain. It rained, and the creek started to rise. The creek, naturally, rises every time it rains; this didn't seem any different. But it kept raining, and, that morning of the twenty-first, the creek kept rising.

That morning I'm standing at my kitchen window. Tinker Creek is out of its four-foot banks, way out, and it's still coming. The high creek doesn't look like our creek. Our creek splashes transparently over a jumble of rocks; the high creek obliterates everything in flat opacity. It looks like somebody else's creek that has usurped or eaten our creek and is roving frantically to escape, big and ugly, like a blacksnake caught in a kitchen drawer. The color is foul, a rusty cream. Water that has picked up clay soils looks worse than other muddy waters because the particles of clay are so fine; they spread out and cloud the water so that you can't see light through even an inch of it in a drinking glass.

Everything looks different. Where my eye is used to depth, I see the flat water, near, too near. I see trees I never noticed before, the black verticals of their rain-soaked trunks standing out of the pale water like pilings for a rotted dock. The stillness of grassy banks and stony ledges is gone; I see rushing, a wild sweep and hurry in one direction, as swift and compelling as a waterfall. The Atkins kids are out in their tiny rain gear, staring at the monster creek. It's risen up to their gates; the neighbors are gathering; I go out.

I hear a roar, a high windy sound more like air than like water, like the run-together whaps of a helicopter's propeller after the engine is off, a high million rushings. The air smells damp and acrid, like fuel oil, or insecticide. It's raining.

I'm in no danger; my house is high. I hurry down the road to the bridge. Neighbors who have barely seen each other all winter are there, shaking their heads. Few have ever seen it before: the water is *over* the bridge. Even when I see the bridge now, which I do every day, I still can't believe it: the water was *over* the bridge, a foot or two over the bridge, which at normal times is eleven feet above the surface of the creek.

Now the water is receding slightly; someone has produced empty metal drums, which we roll to the bridge and set up in a square to keep cars from trying to cross. It takes a bit of nerve even to stand on the bridge; the flood has ripped away a wedge of concrete that buttressed the bridge on the bank. Now one corner of the bridge hangs apparently unsupported while water hurls in an arch just inches below.

It's hard to take it all in, it's all so new. I look at the creek at my feet. It smashes under the bridge like a fist, but there is no end to its force; it hurtles down as far as I can see till it lurches round the bend, filling the valley, flattening, mashing, pushed, wider and faster, till it fills my brain.

It's like a dragon. Maybe it's because the bridge we are on is chancy, but I notice that no one can help imagining himself washed overboard, and gauging his chances for survival. You couldn't live. Mark Spitz couldn't live. The water arches where the bridge's supports at the banks prevent its enormous volume from going wide, forcing it to go high; that arch drives down like a diving whale, and would butt you on the bottom. "You'd never know what hit you," one of the men says. But if you survived that part and managed to surface...? How fast can you live? You'd need a windshield. You couldn't keep your head up; the water under the surface is fastest. You'd spin around like a sock in a clothes dryer. You couldn't grab onto a tree trunk without leaving that arm behind. No, you couldn't live. And if they ever found you, your gut would be solid red clay.

It's all I can do to stand. I feel dizzy, drawn, mauled. Below me the floodwater roils to a violent froth that looks like dirty lace, a lace that continuously explodes before my eyes. If I look away, the earth moves backwards, rises and swells, from the fixing of my eyes at one spot against the motion of the flood. All the familiar land looks as though it were not solid and real at all, but painted on a scroll like a backdrop, and that unrolled scroll has been shaken, so the earth sways and the air roars.

Everything imaginable is zipping by, almost too fast to see. If I stand on the bridge and look downstream, I get dizzy; but if I look upstream, I feel as though I am looking up the business end of an avalanche. There are dolls, split wood and kindling, dead fledgling songbirds, bottles, whole bushes and trees, rakes and garden gloves. Wooden, rough-hewn railroad ties charge by faster than any express. Lattice fencing bobs along, and a wooden picket gate. There are so many white plastic gallon milk jugs that when the flood ultimately recedes, they are left on the grassy banks looking from a distance like a flock of white geese.

I expect to see anything at all. In this one way, the creek is more like itself when it floods than at any other time: mediating, bringing things down. I wouldn't be at all surprised to see John Paul Jones coming round the bend, standing on the deck of the *Bon Homme Richard*, or Amelia Earhart waving gaily from the cockpit of her floating Lockheed. Why not a cello, a basket of breadfruit, a casket of antique coins? Here comes the Franklin expedition on snowshoes, and the three magi, plus camels, afloat on a canopied barge!

The whole world is in flood, the land as well as the water. Water streams down the trunks of trees, drips from hat-brims, courses across roads. The whole earth seems to slide like sand down a chute; water pouring over the least slope leaves the grass flattened, silver side up, pointing downstream. Everywhere windfall and flotsam twigs and leafy boughs, wood from woodpiles, bottles, and saturated straw spatter the ground or streak it in curving windrows. Tomatoes in flat gardens are literally floating in mud; they look as though they have been dropped whole into a boiling, brown-gravy stew. The level of the water table is at the top of the toe of my shoes. Pale muddy water lies on the flat so that it all but drowns the grass; it looks like a hideous parody of a light snow on the field, with only the dark tips of the grass blades visible.

When I look across the street, I can't believe my eyes. Right behind the road's shoulder are waves, waves whipped in rhythmically peaking scallops, racing downstream. The hill where I watched the praying mantis lay her eggs is a waterfall that splashes into a brown ocean. I can't even remember where the creek usually runs – it is everywhere now. My log is gone for sure, I think – but in fact, I discover later, it holds, rammed between growing trees. Only the cable suspending the steers' fence is visible, and not the fence itself; the steers' pasture is entirely in flood, a brown river. The river leaps its banks and smashes into the woods where the motorbikes go, devastating all but the sturdiest trees. The water is so deep and wide it seems as though you could navigate the *Queen Mary* in it, clear to Tinker Mountain.

What do animals do in these floods? I see a drowned muskrat go by like he's flying, but they all couldn't die; the water rises after every hard rain, and the creek is still full of muskrats. This flood is higher than their raised sleeping platforms in the banks; they must just race for high ground and hold on. Where do the fish go, and what do they do? Presumably their gills can filter oxygen out of this muck, but I don't know how. They must hide from the current behind any barriers they can find, and fast for a few days. They must: otherwise we'd have no fish; they'd all be in the Atlantic Ocean. What about herons and kingfishers, say? They can't see to eat. It usually seems to me that when I see any animal, its business is urgent enough that it couldn't easily be suspended for forty-eight hours. Crayfish, frogs, snails, rotifers? Most things must simply die. They couldn't live. Then I suppose that when the water goes down and clears, the survivors have a field day with no competition. But you'd think the bottom would be knocked out of the food chain – the whole pyramid would have no base plankton, and it would crumble, or crash with a thud. Maybe enough spores and larvae and eggs are constantly being borne down from slower upstream waters to repopulate... I don't know.

Some little children have discovered a snapping turtle as big as a tray. It's hard to believe that this creek could support a predator that size: its shell is a foot and a half across, and its head extends a good seven inches beyond the shell. When the children – in the company of a shrunken terrier – approach it on the bank, the snapper rears up on its thick front legs and hisses very impressively. I had read earlier that since turtles' shells are rigid, they don't have bellows lungs; they have to gulp for air. And, also since their shells are rigid, there's only room for so much inside, so when they are frightened and planning a retreat, they have to expel air from their lungs to make room for head and feet – hence the malevolent hiss.

The next time I look, I see that the children have somehow maneuvered the snapper into a washtub. They're waving a broom handle at it in hopes that it will snap the wood like a matchstick, but the creature will not deign to oblige. The kids are crushed; all their lives they've heard that this is the one thing you do with a snapping turtle – you shove a broom handle near it, and it "snaps it like a match-stick." It's nature's way; it's sure-fire. But the turtle is having none of it. It avoids the broom handle with an air of patiently repressed rage. They let it go, and it beelines down the bank, dives unhesitatingly into the swirling floodwater and that's the last we see of it.

A cheer comes up from the crowd on the bridge. The truck is here with a pump for the Bowerys' basement, hooray! We roll away the metal drums, the truck makes it over the bridge, to my amazement – the crowd cheers again. State police cruise by; everything's fine here; downstream people are in trouble. The bridge over by the Bings' on Tinker Creek looks like it's about to go. There's a tree trunk wedged against its railing, and a section of concrete is out. The Bings are away, and a young couple is living there, "taking care of the house." What can they do? The husband drove to work that morning as usual; a few hours later, his wife was evacuated from the front door in a *motorboat*.

I walk to the Bings'. Most of the people who are on our bridge eventually end up over there; it's just down the road. We straggle along in the rain, gathering a crowd. The men who work away from home are here, too; their wives have telephoned them at work this morning to say that the creek is rising fast and they'd better get home while the gettin's good.

There's a big crowd already there; everybody knows that the Bings' is low. The creek is coming in the recreation-room windows; it's halfway up the garage door. Later that day people will haul out everything salvageable and try to dry it: books, rugs, furniture – the lower level was filled from floor to ceiling. Now on this bridge a road crew is trying to chop away the wedged tree trunk with a long-handled ax. The handle isn't so long that they don't have to stand on the bridge, in Tinker Creek. I walk along a low brick wall that was built to retain the creek away from the house at high water. The wall holds just fine, but now that the creek's receding, it's retaining water around the house. On the wall I can walk right out into the flood and stand in the middle of it. Now on the return trip I meet a young man who's going in the opposite direction. The wall is one brick wide; we can't pass. So we clasp hands and lean out backwards over the turbulent water; our feet interlace like teeth on a zipper, we pull together, stand, and continue on our ways. The kids have spotted a rattlesnake draping itself out of harm's way in a bush; now they all want to walk over the brick wall to the bush, to get bitten by the snake.

The little Atkins kids are here, and they are hopping up and down. I wonder if I hopped up and down, would the bridge go? I could stand at the railing as at the railing of a steamboat, shouting deliriously, "Mark three! Quarter-less-three! Half twain! Quarter twain! . . . " as the current bore the broken bridge out of sight around the bend before she sank. . . .

Everyone else is standing around. Some of the women are carrying curious plastic umbrellas that look like diving bells – umbrellas they don't put up, but on;

they don't get under, but in. They can see out dimly, like goldfish in bowls. Their voices from within sound distant, but with an underlying cheerfulness that plainly acknowledges, "Isn't this ridiculous?" Some of the men are wearing their fishing hats. Others duck their heads under folded newspapers held not very high in an effort to compromise between keeping their heads dry and letting rain run up their sleeves. Following some form of courtesy, I guess, they lower these newspapers when they speak with you, and squint politely into the rain.

Women are bringing coffee in mugs to the road crew. They've barely made a dent in the tree trunk, and they're giving up. It's a job for power tools; the water's going down anyway and the danger is past. Some kid starts doing tricks on a skateboard; I head home.

★   ★   ★

On the same day that I was standing on bridges here over Tinker Creek, a friend, Lee Zacharias, was standing on a bridge in Richmond over the James River. It was a calm day there, with not a cloud in the skies. The James River was up a mere nine feet, which didn't look too unusual. But floating in the river was everything under the bright sun. As Lee watched, chicken coops raced by, chunks of houses, porches, stairs, whole uprooted trees – and finally a bloated dead horse. Lee knew, all of Richmond knew: it was coming.

There the James ultimately rose thirty-two feet. The whole town was under water, and all the electrical power was out. When Governor Holton signed the emergency relief bill – which listed our county among the federal disaster areas – he had to do it by candlelight.

That night a curious thing happened in the blacked-out Governor's mansion. Governor Holton walked down an upstairs hall and saw, to his disbelief, a lightbulb glowing in a ceiling fixture. It was one of three bulbs, all dead – the whole city was dead – but that one bulb was giving off a faint electrical light. He stared at the thing, scratched his head, and summoned an electrician. The electrician stared at the thing, scratched his head, and announced, "Impossible." The governor went back to bed, and the electrician went home. No explanation has ever been found.

★   ★   ★

Later Agnes would move on up into Maryland, Pennsylvania, and New York, killing people and doing hundreds of millions of dollars worth of damage. Here in Virginia alone it killed twelve people and ruined 166 million dollars worth of property. But it hit Pennsylvania twice, coming and going. I talked to one of the helicopter pilots who had helped airlift ancient corpses from a flooded cemetery in Wilkes-Barre, Pennsylvania. The flood left the bodies stranded on housetops, in trees; the pilots, sickened, had to be relieved every few hours. The one I talked to, in a little sandwich shop at the Peaks of Otter on the Blue Ridge Parkway, preferred Vietnam. We were lucky here.

* * *

This winter I heard a final flood story, about an extra dividend that the flood left the Bings, a surprise as unexpected as a baby in a basket on a stoop.

The Bings came home and their house was ruined, but somehow they managed to salvage almost everything, and live as before. One afternoon in the fall a friend went to visit them; as he was coming in, he met a man coming out, a professor with a large volume under his arm. The Bings led my friend inside and into the kitchen, where they proudly opened the oven door and showed him a giant mushroom – which they were baking to serve to guests the following day. The professor with the book had just been verifying its edibility. I imagined the mushroom, wrinkled, black, and big as a dinner plate, erupting overnight mysteriously in the Bings' living room – from the back of an upholstered couch, say, or from a still-damp rug under an armchair.

Alas, the story as I had fixed it in my mind proved to be only partly true. The Bings often cook wild mushrooms, and they know what they're doing. This particular mushroom had grown outside, under a sycamore, on high ground that the flood hadn't touched. So the flood had nothing to do with it. But it's still a good story, and I like to think that the flood left them a gift, a consolation prize, so that for years to come they will be finding edible mushrooms here and there about the house, dinner on the bookshelf, hors d'oeuvres in the piano. It would have been nice.

From Pilgrim at Tinker Creek. *Used by permission of the Author.*

Annie Dillard is the author of a book of poems, Tickets for a Prayer Wheel; *a prose narrative,* Holy the Firm; *a book of literary theory,* Living by Fiction; *a collection of personal narratives,* Teaching a Stone to Talk; *an account,* Encounters with Chinese Writers; *a memoir,* An American Childhood; *and* Pilgrim at Tinker Creek, *which was awarded the Pulitzer Prize.*

Peter S. Felknor

NOT VERY LONG AGO, the average person would probably think of *The Wizard of Oz* when challenged to describe a tornado. Myths and fallacies abounded: packing winds of "thousands" of miles per hour, tornadoes were famed for feats like hurling two-by-fours through solid steel or turning cast-iron kettles inside out. Inhabiting a spectral shadow zone just this side of Sasquatches and space aliens, these small but violent storms seemed always to happen to other people, most of whom lived in trailer parks.

The advent of the video camcorder changed all that. Suddenly the tornado arrived in the American living room. Bankers in office towers, young recruits on military bases, terrified motorists on Midwestern highways all turned their video cameras toward the sky. A new cadre of dedicated thrill seekers evolved, known as storm chasers, and in just a couple of years the backroads of Texas and Oklahoma filled up with freshly minted tornado buffs who hunted "the classic wedge tornado" the way their forebears had stalked big game on the very same plains.

Soon enough, Hollywood weighed in with *Twister*. The big-money entertainment interests had decided that it was safe to gamble on a fanciful film about a bunch of scientific misfits who chase tornadoes for a living. In the 1980s this would have been unthinkable; by 1996 it spelled enormous box-office success. Never mind that Dr. Howard Bluestein, the man who had tried years earlier to drop an instrument package called TOTO (the Totable Tornado Observatory) in a tornado's damage path, had long since gone on to more productive if less glamorous pursuits. *Twister* had the atmosphere, the romance, the special effects – and who really cared if, meteorologically speaking, it was a hoot?

It's hard to imagine that even twenty years ago, American tornado researchers were routinely met with blank stares or jokes about Auntie Em. It's harder still to believe that we must travel much farther back in time, to the raw American frontier of 1879, to discover the origins of modern tornado science.

Settlers on the Great Plains led the most difficult of lives. Often believing that the West offered a utopia they would never find in the forest glades of Connecticut or the salt marshes of Virginia, they uprooted their families with visions of an agrarian horn of plenty on the vast prairies – a notion very much encouraged by their government. Instead they found locusts, drought, and a decided lack of popularity with their Native American neighbors. And, of course, they found tornadoes.

During that era, the Army was the chief federal agency overseeing the Plains states, and it was still embroiled in conflicts between Indian tribes and the growing ranks of white settlers (Custer had made his Last Stand only three years earlier). Next to nothing was known about the violent tempests that were yet another hazard of life on the plains. When wide areas of Kansas, Missouri, Iowa, and Nebraska were raked by severe tornadoes in May 1879, it fell to a young buck private in the United States Army Signal Service to investigate.

John Park Finley was a burly, mustached man of considerable stamina and intellectual resources. His orders were to travel by horse and foot through the remote areas that had sustained wind damage and to issue a report. The Army wanted an idea of how much emergency assistance was needed by the scattered homesteaders and whether it might be possible to prevent such a disaster from happening again. A soldier always determined to do his best, even in nearly impossible circumstances, young Finley was sent on his way.

Scraping the mud from his boots after returning from the scene, Finley scripted a terse letter to his commanding officers:

While pursuing my labors [there were] unexpected and unusual difficulties: almost incessant rains, accompanied by some of the most severe wind and hail storms that ever visited the Lower Missouri Valley. Hardly three days out of an entire month was the weather at all pleasant or conducive to good work. Bridges were washed away, streams swollen to rushing rivers, and roads turned into soft, sinking morasses, almost impassable to man or beast, yet in twenty days I traveled over 500 miles with horse and buggy, and also did considerable walking...

Finley's report must have staggered his superiors. Titled *Tornadoes of May 29th and 30th, 1879*, it was at once a concise reporting job and a fully realized book, laced with Finley's compassion for the horror and suffering he had witnessed, as well as an engineer's astounding eye for physical detail. Finley did more than just put facts on paper; he was a consummate interviewer and a devoted wordsmith. He set the standard for generations of later researchers in the documentation of windstorms.

He began with a rather amazing synopsis of the weather conditions that had preceded the tornado outbreak. Hampered by limited knowledge of the upper atmosphere (radiosonde balloons were unknown at the time) and lacking even a solid body of meteorological theory, Finley still did a respectable job of isolating the large-scale atmospheric conditions that give rise to tornado formation: the marked temperature and moisture differentials on either side of a cold front trailing southward from a deep low pressure area; the veering wind profiles that enable large thunderstorms to begin to rotate and to spawn tornadoes; and even the existence of a powerful jet stream overhead, which Finley had deduced (without really knowing it) from the fact that strong storms throughout the month had continually traveled along similar paths, "becoming thereby the principal factor in the work of inducing this unusual movement of [unstable] air to the north."

But the centerpiece of Finley's book was unquestionably his blow-by-blow description of the nearly complete destruction of Irving, Kansas. An isolated hamlet in the valley of the Big Blue River, Irving suffered the singular misfortune of being struck by two tornadoes within a half hour. What the first storm had started, the second finished with demonic furor; by all accounts, the second Irving tornado reduced the stoutest hearts to terror.

As a young boy, I had been overwhelmed by a brief quotation from Finley's Irving account that had appeared in a popular book on natural disasters. The quotation was wrongly attributed, and quite a few years went by before I discovered the real author. It took me still more years to locate Finley's book but I finally found it, buried deep in the dusts of a New York City historical archive. I flipped through the yellowed pages, past a series of fantastically detailed hand-drawn maps of Irving and environs, until my eye settled upon a description of the tornado Finley called "Irving Storm No. 1."

*There was observed forming in the southwest and northwest about 5 p.m.,
dark, heavy clouds. Their appearance was considered nothing unusual except
that they came up very suddenly, first from the northwest and then the southwest.
In fact, a storm was rather expected, because of the sultry and close condition of
the atmosphere, which had continued most of the day with a southerly wind. In a
short time the clouds which had come up so quickly and quietly were thrown into
the most terrible commotion; huge black masses, mingled with lighter clouds,
would roll upward in front of and between the opposing currents, the latter sometimes shooting upward with lightning velocity. Rain and large hail had already
commenced to fall, and in about fifteen minutes the whirlwind of destruction
formed, having the shape of a huge elephant's trunk, and gradually lowered itself
towards the ground ...*

Storm No. 1 first touched down at Bala, about 40 miles southwest of Irving and
very close to the present-day Fort Riley. A classic Plains cyclone with an unmistakable
funnel cloud, No. 1 had already claimed several lives when it roared down a prairie
divide west of Irving and smashed into the town. Following what could be considered a fortuitous route along the settlement's southern fringes, the tornado destroyed
several houses and caused quite a few serious injuries before it turned to follow the
course of the Big Blue. Now the swirling vortex swiftly dispatched the city's new
iron bridge – lifting it from its support saddles, twisting the girders and rods into
metallic spaghetti, and unceremoniously dumping the whole mess into the river.

*The sun, now partially exposed beneath the heavy clouds lining the western
horizon, threw its warm rays upon the terror-stricken inhabitants, who, at this
welcome visitation, assuring them, as they thought, of peace and protection,
emerged from their cellars and "dug-outs" to witness the destruction already com-
mitted and relieve their suffering neighbors.*

*Hardly had the people recovered from the first shock, when there appeared in
the west a cloud of inky blackness and enormous dimensions, presenting a square
front of apparently two miles in width and a perpendicular height from earth
to sky. It moved along slowly, but with the most inconceivable majesty of force,
apparently annihilating everything within its reach.*

*No funnel-shaped cloud was noticed during its passage through the town, and
but little commotion or tumbling of the clouds until it commenced its work of
destruction, first, upon the farm of Mr. Preston, one mile northwest of the city,
which it reached about 6:20 p.m. His buildings were only partially destroyed, as
they were situated on the western edge of the storm, on a rise of ground above the
valley, yet not upon the high prairie. From this point to the defenceless [sic] town
there was nothing but a wide sweep of prairie grass. The town is now reached,
and as the awful cloud starts upon its frightful mission of death and destruction*

it strikes into a cluster of eighteen houses and other buildings, within a radius of less than half a mile. Nearly all were swept to the earth in terrible ruin ...

A disturbing trend among the current crop of storm chasers and tornado enthusiasts is a marked lack of concern about the human costs of tornadoes. *Twister*, to its credit, did briefly portray for its millions of viewers the grim aftermath of a tornado's nighttime assault on an Oklahoma town. But Finley was never able to separate his fascination for his subject from the havoc and trauma left behind, and he returned from his fieldwork on the Great Plains a changed man.

As the terrible scene of desolation was approached the cries of wounded people and the moans of the tortured animals were plainly heard, which, mingled with the distant roar of the storm, filled one with an indescribable fear and dread of the awful monster that was still in sight, and was a fearful reminder of its terrific force.

Upon arriving at the ruins of the once happy home a dreadful sight was presented. Human beings could not be distinguished from animals as all alike were covered with mud and mingled with an interminable mass of debris in the most sickening manner. Women and children stripped of their clothing were found lying by the side of horses and hogs. Now an arm or a leg would be raised up from the filthy mess surrounding them, attended with a piercing shriek for help, and upon examination ugly gaping wounds were found filled with mud, straw and bits of wood ...

The more I read into Finley's work the more I saw what an incredible feat he had accomplished. Not only had he singlehandedly invented the science of the tornado damage survey, he had also boldly struck out into uncharted territory both literally and figuratively, beginning to piece together the riddle of the tornado while never losing sight of the unique emotional costs of a natural disaster.

Still remembering the profound impact his impressions had had on me as a child, I resolved to travel to Irving myself, to stand where Finley had stood and to see – or at least to imagine – what he had seen.

★   ★   ★

On a beautiful April morning, I followed the empty highway northward from Manhattan, Kansas, where I had spent the night. My mission was to find Irving, but it appeared in none of my several travel atlases. Finley had located the town about five miles southeast of Blue Rapids, on the right bank of the Big Blue. Nowadays, much of the Blue Valley of Finley's day lies submerged beneath Tuttle Creek Lake, formed when the Army Corps of Engineers dammed the Big Blue just above Manhattan (some 40 miles south of Irving). From modern maps, it appeared that the reservoir's northern terminus was very near the site of Irving. Perhaps I would find a handful of hangers-on, maybe only a watery grave. Finding the "pleasant and thriving village" that Finley had described seemed out of the question.

I was fortunate to have brought along one of Finley's fanatically precise maps of the area; I made my way north, ticking off the miles to Irving by the location of waterways, all nicely demarcated by the Kansas Highway Department: Fancy Creek, Swede Creek, Game Fork Creek. Just over the Marshall County line, past the hamlet of Randolph – which the first Irving tornado had narrowly missed – I knew I had to turn east, back toward the reservoir.

At a junction marked only by a garage, I left the highway. Crawling eastward along a gravel road, I watched as the land turned strange and haunted. The earth seemed to have been scoured clean. The few trees, planted in lonely beachheads around farms likely as not to have been abandoned long ago, were bent over from the incessant southerly winds. Without their leaves, they looked forlorn and arthritic.

Some of these farmsteads had probably been in the path of Storm No. 1. I tried to picture the darkening skies, the crazy clouds rushing toward each other on the horizon. It was difficult; this day was too perfect. The only dark cloud was my memory of the awful things Finley had witnessed here.

After eight miles of gravel road, I descended the "high divide" into the Blue Valley. I was stunned to find no sign of Tuttle Creek Lake. I gazed across the vast, verdant sweep of the land. Everything was pristine and picture-perfect; I easily imagined myself regarding this vista with the weary but optimistic eye of a German or Czech immigrant farmer, my family waiting in the wagon behind me. *This is the place.* On a day like today, the Blue Valley looked a lot like the Garden of Eden.

And then, 20 years after these poor farmers and traders had settled there, Irving was erased from the earth in a scene more reminiscent of the biblical destruction of Sodom and Gomorrah. Finley interviewed a Mr. Charles Preston, proprietor of a seminary at Irving, who graphically described his experiences during the passage of Storm No. 2:

> *Our first sensations upon the contact of the storm were as though the building had been picked up, violently shaken, and then set down again. The next instant the doors and windows were broken in, the furniture whirled around the room and broken in pieces, and I, standing in the E. room, picked up, whirled around, and carried through the folding doors into the main school-room to the W. and laid upon the floor uninjured.*
>
> *The same instant the S. end of the building was carried away and most of the roof disappeared. Upon rising from the floor I found my clothing torn into shreds, but not a bruise upon my body. While in the act of taking hold of a door-knob to descend into the basement, where I had sent my family, I found both hands benumbed as though asleep, and I was unable to open the door, while my wrists, elbows, and shoulder-blades felt more like the effects from the shock of a galvanic battery, yet no lightning was seen in the cloud or about it during its passage.*
>
> *During the passage of the storm, electricity ran over the walls of my house, throwing off sparks like an emery wheel; but of a paler color; yet I would*

attribute this effect to the particles of sand and plaster blown from the walls by the extreme violence of the wind. While standing in the school-room, from the floor of which I had risen, I saw through the open doors and windows to the E. the flight of the storm. The cloud was of such intense blackness that I could not see anything of the buildings it would envelop, but as the milky mist passed away, which seemed to linger over the ruins, the terrible work was brought to light.

I had reached a dead end. The gravel road dropped into the valley, then made an abrupt turn toward the north. I knew that when I approached the river, I should be very close to Irving – or whatever was left of it. But I could not get to the river without turning east again.

Ahead of me was a low shrubby woods, growing up along a path running east and west. To my left was the high divide and a lonely windmill silhouetted against the spotless backdrop of the sky. I glanced to my right, and was surprised to see a tiny private cemetery, a miniature greensward clustered around a single, imposing tombstone.

I looked closer. The tombstone said **IRVING**. I had arrived.

Walking into the woods across the path from the tombstone, I noticed a pungent, rank smell. The forest had caught fire recently, probably during an electrical storm. Before I had gone very far, my shoes scraped across something foreign: cement! There had even been sidewalks here; now they vanished into impossibly tangled underbrush. This was unlike the other ghost towns I had visited. In those towns no one, it seemed, had had the time or the inclination to install cement sidewalks. Irving, as Finley had said, must have been a rather civilized place in its day – lacking, perhaps, the amenities and frills of Kansas City or St. Joseph, but a beautiful setting in which to watch the sun set, surrounded by friendly neighbors, cooperative soil, and a sky without end.

A clearing in the brush made itself out to be a road – or, more precisely, a street. The shapes of foundations began to emerge through the trees. I felt as if I had stumbled upon the ruins of Herculaneum or Pompeii, but with an added pang of wistfulness. People abandoned towns for all sorts of reasons. Usually they just up and left, following the promise of greener pastures or the lure of easier money. That was human nature. But Irving, with its sad remnants of a former contentment – here a half-buried washtub, there a flower garden encircling a tidy foundation – suggested only tragedy. The paths that had once been streets wound through the woods, busily intersecting each other, drifting off to the same dead ends that had awaited the long-ago settlers who had so laboriously constructed these stone foundations. No one was here to remember. I was alone with what I knew.

The path I followed, which had once been known as Raymond Street, opened out into a clearing and descended a steep hill. At the bottom of the hill was the old course of the Big Blue, now devoid of even a trickle of water and choked with underbrush. I was not far from the site of a former bridge; pieces of lumber still lay embedded in the old river mud. Beneath my feet were bricks, strewn across a sloping field. I could gaze for miles up the valley toward the northwest. Suddenly I felt suffocated and had to fight the urge to turn around and leave. In an instant I had figured out exactly where I was.

> *...With a roar like that of a thousand cannons, the cloud covered the little town.*

This was where Storm No. 2 had claimed its victims, this gradual rise of land leading into Irving from the north and west. Here entire streets of flimsy frame houses had been lifted up, shredded, and smashed into the earth, the hapless settlers within meeting the same fate. The place had the peculiar oppressiveness found at the site of great battles or concentration camps. The horrible semicircular sweep of the field was littered with bricks and branches, seemingly incapable of supporting life.

It was a beautiful day. I couldn't wait to get out of there.

The foundations and flower gardens remained blissfully heedless as I trekked back through Irving's aimless, deserted avenues. Where I had left my car, at the former commercial intersection of Main and Jerome streets, there was nothing but the wind pushing down from Finley's high divide. The wind bore that springtime aroma of new beginnings, of pollen and freshly turned earth. Only the incongruity of the tombstone across the road – once the cornerstone of City Hall, I was to discover – hinted that there would be no more beginnings in Irving.

I drove up the divide and out of the valley. A pair of cardinals careened over the road in happy pursuit; I realized that I had heard no birds in Irving. Back here on the high prairie, the sun smiled down and the early crops waved in a gentle breeze, and one could have imagined that it had always been this way. Many things had changed in Kansas since the settlers had reached the Blue Valley in 1859, but certainly the sky had not. The sky had swallowed the settlers; today it remembered nothing.

(Quotations are from *Tornadoes of May 29th and 30th, 1879* by John Park Finley. Washington, D.C.: U.S. Department of War, Professional Papers of the Signal Service, no. 4. U.S. Government Printing Office, 1881.)

Peter Felknor is a native of Missouri where he developed his childhood interest in tornadoes (and the work of John Park Finley). He is a graduate of the University of Wisconsin-Madison where he studied meteorology and environmental risk assessment. He is the author of The Tri-State Tornado *and several journal articles about tornado disasters.*

The Shape of Air

Chet Raymo

I spend part of each year in a house on a hill in the west of Ireland. The place is truly a castle in the air. The view out of every window is atmospheric, ever changing, an operatic play of wind, water vapor, and light. We have no television. There, the drama of the air is entertainment enough. I have never visited any other place with so much weather – hailstones the size of marbles thumping on the slates; mists rolling through the mountain pass like molasses; rainbows out the bedroom window in the afternoons; stars glimpsed through heaped masses of moonlit cloud; soft days (as the Irish say) and days of raging gales.

This is the earth at its living best, Gaia gauzed in furl and flurry. The movements of the crustal plates that transform the rocky surface of the earth are too slow to be observed on the human scale. Currents that stir the seas are mostly hidden by depth and opacity. But in the atmosphere, Gaia flaunts her vivacity, allowing us enough transparency to observe great expanses of air, yet revealing her movements with signatures of cloud. What I observe from the windows of my house in Ireland is nothing less than the animated earth, starkly manifest.

What is the air? Thoreau, in one of his more rhapsodic moments, called it a "foundry full of molds for casting bluebirds' warbles." His flamboyant image lends itself to meteorological analysis. The subtle warps and crevices of air, defined by temperature, by pressure and movement, can indeed give shape to sound, teasing a bluebird's call far out across a summer meadow, or slurring the vibrancy of the warble. Similarly, air gives shape to light, life, and spirit. "The air," said Thoreau, "is as deep as our natures."

Physically, however, the air is less deep than we are likely to believe. Wrap a bowling ball in a single layer of clear kitchen wrap and you have a pretty good scale model of the earth and its atmosphere. Within that wisp-thin envelope are all of the phenomena of air: the tumbling clouds, the bluebird's call, the flights of kites and dragonflies, rainbows, hurricanes, pea soup fogs, the flicker of fireflies and the hoots of owls, acrid smogs, scarlet sunsets.

The only problem with the kitchen wrap model is that the atmosphere has no well-defined upper boundary. The planet's gassy envelope yields with increasing tenuousness to the vacuum of space; in other words, it gets thinner and thinner until it isn't there anymore. Nevertheless, once we have ascended ten miles above the earth's surface – or about the thickness of the kitchen wrap compared to the bowling ball – most of the atmosphere is below us.

The lower ten miles or so of the atmosphere is called the troposphere, from the Greek *tropos*, for "change" or "turn." Within this shell, temperatures decrease with altitude, dropping as low as minus eighty degrees Fahrenheit near the top. These temperature variations and the rotation of the earth set up global movements of air that cause our weather.

Above the troposphere, in the stratosphere, ultraviolet radiation from the sun warms the air, causing the temperature thirty miles or so above the surface to reach a relatively balmy sixty-five degrees Fahrenheit. This is the realm of ozone, a form of oxygen that absorbs the sun's ultraviolet radiation, protecting life on the surface from deadly short-wavelength light. Here, too, cosmic rays (high energy particles from space) collide with air molecules and splatter into showers of less energetic – and less harmful – secondary particles. The stratosphere is mostly cloud free, and therefore virtually invisible, but it provides life with indispensable protection against dangers from space.

Above the stratosphere, in the mesosphere (at altitudes of thirty to fifty miles), the temperature plummets again. This is where most meteors burn up, heated by friction with rarefied air, creating those streaks of burning vapor we call "shooting stars." Wisps of ice crystals in the upper mesosphere sometimes catch rays of sunlight after darkness has fallen on the surface, shining with a pale ethereal light – the so-called noctilucent ("night-shining") clouds.

Another reversal of temperature occurs in the thermosphere, above fifty miles, where exceedingly thin air is heated by solar radiation to temperatures of thousands of degrees. Atoms are stripped of electrons by radiation, creating charged ions that affect long-distance radio communication. Here, too, energetic particles streaming from the sun collide with molecules of air, exciting them to luminescence and igniting spectacular auroral displays near the earth's poles.

The thermosphere extends to several hundred miles above the surface – about a quarter of an inch above the surface of the bowling ball – to the realm of low-orbiting satellites. This is the threshold of space and, for all practical purposes, the top of the atmosphere.

Every layer of atmosphere contributes to our well-being; every layer enhances the visual beauty of the sky.

What we can't observe from the earth's surface is the kitchen-wrap thinness of the atmosphere. On the human scale, the atmosphere seems to reach to the stars, a vast and inviolable munificence of air. Photographs of the earth from space reveal a different picture. We see the planet on its own scale, suspended in the inky dark of space, skinned with cloud. How fragile the atmosphere appears in the space photographs, how wispy thin. Only the gentle tug of gravity holds it to the surface, against the tendency of gas to expand into a vacuum.

The earth acquired its atmosphere at its fiery beginning. Then, more than four billion years ago, the planet was mostly molten, or almost so – a planet-encompassing volcano. From the seething surface bubbled up the gasses that became the first atmosphere. It is likely that the earth's earliest atmosphere was similar to the present atmospheres of our neighboring planets, but that situation no longer prevails. The atmospheres of Venus and Mars have large components of carbon dioxide and almost no oxygen. The earth's atmosphere is one-fifth oxygen and almost no carbon dioxide. The difference is due to the presence on the earth of two things – liquid water and life.

Carbon dioxide readily combines with water to form carbonic acid. Carbonic acid in solution loses its hydrogen and combines with calcium and magnesium to form insoluble carbonates. These carbonates precipitate into bottom sediments that harden into the rocks we know as limestone and dolomite. Animals and plants in the sea take up carbonates to build their skeletons and shells. At death, these also fall to the bottom of the sea as part of rock-forming sediments. If you are looking for the carbon dioxide from the earth's earliest atmosphere, you will find it in these sediments – in the limestone quarries of Indiana or the chalky white cliffs of Dover.

And what about the oxygen? Where did the oxygen in the earth's atmosphere come from? Some results from the breakup of water molecules in the upper atmosphere by ultraviolet light (the hydrogen subsequently escaping into space). But most of the oxygen was contributed by life, as a by-product of photosynthesis. Blue-green bacteria that lived in the earth's early oceans manufactured the air we breathe as they turned sunlight into sugar. Plants continue the process today.

For a billion years, the atmosphere has been in balance with animals, plants, sea, and rocks. The gasses of the air are cycled and recycled through the earth's crust, oceans, and biosphere, in a kind of breath that resembles our own. It is a grand engine, or metabolism, depending on whether you prefer a mechanical or a biological metaphor. It is an ongoing process, delicately tuned, adjusting itself with the deliberate languor of evolution.

As I watch the voluminous heavings of air from the window of my Irish hilltop house, it is difficult to imagine that any human activity might change the product of eons. But none of us should doubt the capacity of life to impose its nature upon the air; one need only compare the earth's atmosphere with the atmospheres of Mars or Venus. What is new is technology, which amplifies the speed of atmospheric change, outpacing the capacity of geological process or biological evolution to adapt, disrupting a balance patiently contrived at Gaia's own unhurried pace.

The Greek word *pneuma* can be translated as "wind," "breath," or "spirit." The atmosphere is all that. It is *pneuma*. It is *tropos*. It is kitchen-wrap thin. It is a foundry for bluebirds' warbles. It is the medium of voice, of song, and music. It is the breeze of a summer's day. It is the breath of life. And, as Thoreau said, it is as deep as our nature.

Reprinted from Sanctuary Magazine, *Massachusetts Audubon Society, by permission of the publisher.*

Chet Raymo is a writer, teacher, and naturalist who explores the relationship between science, nature, and religion. He is the author of eleven books, including Skeptics and True Believers; The Soul of the Night: An Astronomical Pilgrimage; Honey from Stone: A Naturalist's Search for God; *and* 365 Starry Nights. *Chet Raymo lives in Massachusetts, where he teaches physics and astronomy at Stonehill College and writes a science column for the* Boston Globe.

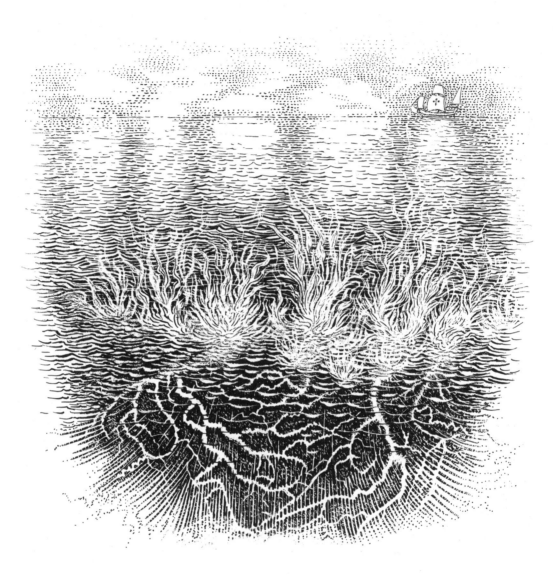

Gretel Ehrlich

Selected from *A Match to the Heart*

DEEP IN AN OCEAN. I am suspended motionless. The water is gray. That's all there is, and before that? My arms are held out straight, cruciate, my head and legs hang limp. Nothing moves. Brown kelp lies flat in mud and fish are buried in liquid clouds of dust. There are no shadows or sounds. Should there be? I don't know if I am alive, but if not, how do I know I am dead? My body is leaden, heavier than gravity.

Gravity is done with me. No more sinking and rising or bobbing in currents. There is a terrible feeling of oppression with no oppressor. I try to lodge my mind against some boundary, some reference point, but the continent of the body dissolves ...

A single heartbeat stirs gray water. Blue trickles in, just a tiny stream. Then a long silence.

Another heartbeat. This one is louder, as if amplified. Sound takes a shape: it is a snowplow moving grayness aside like a heavy snowdrift. I can't tell if I'm moving, but more blue water flows in. Seaweed begins to undulate, then a whole kelp forest rises from the ocean floor. A fish swims past and looks at me. Another heartbeat drives through dead water, and another, until I am surrounded by blue.

Sun shines above all this. There is no pattern to the way its glint comes free and falls in long knives of light. My two beloved dogs appear. They flank me like tiny rockets, their fur pressed against my ribs. A leather harness holds us all together. The dogs climb toward light, pulling me upward at a slant from the sea.

I have been struck by lightning and I am alive.

* * *

"Fire is not following you, you are following fire," Takashi Masaki, a Japanese farmer-monk admonished me. Was this ocean into which I had fallen a blue flame? For six months actual fires had been breaking out all around me. A plane caught on fire on the runway in Denver and when we leapt to the ground from the stairs and began running – as per instructions – upwind from the plane, the fire engines almost ran over us. A month later the Dallas hotel I was forced to stay in because of another delayed plane burst into flames as I entered the lobby. In June several IRA bomb scares in the London tube sent me dashing up steep stairs to the street. And in July the spruce forest that flanked the runway at Fairbanks erupted as my plane landed and for two weeks the skies of interior Alaska were smoke-gray.

"How does it feel to have fire enter you?" another friend asked after hearing of my accident. I had no answer. Nothing of the incident remained in my retrievable memory. All the cultural references I knew showed gods throwing lightning bolts, not ingesting them, but like the young fire-eaters I'd seen as a child, stationed on the sidewalks of the Paseo de la Reforma in Mexico City, I had swallowed fire.

Lightning is a massive electrical discharge occurring in the atmosphere of the earth, as well as on several planets, and can extend from five to ten kilometers in length. There are about 1,800 thunderstorms in progress over the earth every moment and lightning hits the planet one hundred times each second. In the continental United States alone, there are forty million cloud-to-ground strikes each year.

The life of a 20,000-foot-high cumulonimbus cloud is about twelve hours. It is a city of turrets and towers made out of polygonal convection cells whose interiors are all warm air rushing upward and whose skins are moving walls of cold air. The cumulonimbus is all motion, made of raw energy and mist.

The earth radiates solar energy, warming air, which rises and expands as atmospheric pressure decreases. Taking on altitude, it gives up heat for height. The water inside the cloud condenses and droplets hang on particles of dust. That is how a thundercloud is made. It is a community of cells organized into weather factories in which rain, hail, and snow are dropped to earth, and in which lightning occurs.

Heat and cold, water and dust, that's all it is at inception, but trouble brews. A thundercloud grows unruly, as all cities do, when the shearing stresses between ascending and descending air – as with the wealthy and the poor – result in turbulence. In addition, when dense dry air from outside the cloud is displaced by the updraft, it mixes with saturated air, thus providing a constant supply of recently warmed air full of moisture. This is fed to the upwardly mobile tower. Once begun, the cloud builds on itself, sometimes rising 40,000 feet in the air.

All summer these stately empires sail above Wyoming mountains, processions of cool heads, but inside they are dynamic, chaotic districts drawn into existence by jets of buoyant air, growing in volume and height until they bump into the upper reaches of the stratosphere. Even then, they sometimes continue upward, their turrets penetrating stable layers of air until they can go no further, then they fall back on themselves.

This is only the beginning of the violence a thunderstorm accrues. Benjamin Franklin brought lightning down out of the sky with a kite, a string, and a key. His kite was the object the cloud's electrical charge so desperately sought. Thunderclouds are Hegelian: Electrons and protons are charged particles surrounded by an electrical field that attracts charges of the opposite sign.

Inside the misty cloud-bubble, collisions occur. According to Earle Williams, an MIT geophysicist who gives seminars on lightning, a storm's convection carries water into the cold cloudtop, where it freezes into graupel. Moved vertically, these icy bits collide with other forms of moisture and the friction generates both negative and positive charges.

A thundercloud grows in a state of imbalance. Polarities change back and forth within the cloud as well as on the ground, where the earth's negative charge flips to one that is positive as the storm approaches. Soon, everything is humming with electricity, even individual raindrops. The chaotic acceleration of charge separation taking place divides the cloud into opposing territories that end in a tripole form, a plus-minus-plus structure, like a villanelle, with a strong positive at the top and bottom and, in between, a pancake-shaped region of negative charge.

For a short time the insulating capacity of air prevents the two attracted charges from meeting, but any upright object in the force field becomes a finger that reaches up, straining to touch the other. So loaded is the cloud with electricity, that its negative charge tears a path through the air, stripping off electrons and leaving in its wake positive ions. In the newly carved channel, a sudden flow of electricity slurries down. All this has taken a fraction of a second.

But lightning is not a one-way street. As soon as its tip nears the favored object or area, upward-moving discharges, called "return leader strokes," fly up to an ionized path traveling a third or more times the speed of light. When the return stroke has ceased to flow, another dart leader may drop down, in turn initiating a second return stroke, and so on. Contrary to popular belief, lightning loves to strike the same place twice, since it always follows the path of least resistance. What could be handier than reusing this ionized channel?

The Navajo word for thunder is *I'ni*, meaning "that which moans indefinitely." When the lightning stroke goes back up from the ground, the current surges to 100,000 amperes, or 100 million watts per meter of channel, and the temperature rises to 30,000° K. This heated air causes gases to expand in the discharge channel and a shock wave is sent traveling, quickly decaying into an acoustical wave whose signal, or "signature," is what we call thunder.

Thunder is nature's unique percussion symphony. Pliny wrote in A.D. 77 that it was unsafe to speak of certain kinds of thunder, or even listen to it, lest it bring bad luck. On the other hand, he also noted that Romans used thunder as a tool of divination to predict events, and listened to it to hear secret messages.

We now know that thunder's wavelength is determined by the length, duration, and total energy of the lightning stroke. Instead of reading thunder to know our fortunes, we use it to "read" lightning. For example, the lower the pitch of the thunder, the more powerful the lightning strike has been.

The violence and energy produced by a thunderstorm starts as a spark, then many sparks conjoined and flowing as if seeking to illuminate a dark patch of ground or make incandescent every window of a darkened city with its sudden, ephemeral light. The electricity inside a cloud sweeps back and forth, up and down, always seeking the path of least resistance, while the dynamics of convection works like a heart, pumping air and moisture up through the valve of the cloud and pushing electricity down through an artery. Nothing is ghostlier than lightning's light: pale, colorless, it serves up frozen instants, then disassembles those phantasms and delivers them back to darkness.

* * *

We swim in an ocean of air, in magnetospheric, ionospheric, and tropospheric currents bound together by a global electrical circuit. The surface of the earth gives off a negative charge, which is met equally by a positive atmospheric charge whose conductivity increases with altitude. Galactic cosmic rays bring positive and negative ions into the earth's atmosphere but it is thunderstorms that generate huge amounts of electricity. They are the factories that keep the global circuits going.

There are intracloud, intercloud, and cloud-to-air flashes – heat and sheet lightning, discharges that never touch the earth. Rocket lightning sends horizontal sprays of light across the tops of windblown clouds, and ribbon lightning's stroke is one that has been separated in the channel by wind, thus giving off a double image; cloud-to-ground lightning (the kind that struck me) breaks into luminous fragments, like a necklace of pearls, but no name has been given to the wild lightning that zigzags in all directions at once.

Ball lightning is controversial, often being discounted the way UFO sightings are, because it is not scientifically understood. Are these luminous globes a brew of storm chemicals (oxygen, hydrogen, and nitrogen) or a "brush discharge" – atmospheric electricity bound together somehow? Or is it a collision of charged dust particles, raindrops, and ions? Sightings of these glowing spheres have been recorded continually from ancient times, as crazy, rolling emanations kicked down from the heavens or from some Jovian beach, sometimes bouncing, sometimes rolling down chimneys or slipping into open windows and disappearing under beds like fiery dust motes. They can move fast or slow, hesitating before they roll, and they can either move against a wind, in defiance of physics, or go with the flow. Not rolling stones, they are bodiless, centerless, with no hard nuclei around which sparks can spin, yet they hiss and sparkle and appear, interchangeably, as balls of gold, blue, white, green, or red. Intensely bright to the human eye, they are often "cold," or else hot, as in the case of Diane of France, who on her wedding night, in 1557, saw a ball of light pass around her bedroom in an erratic course, finally bouncing onto her covers and burning her clothes and hair.

A "fire dragon" is what Gregory of Tours called it. But as he had already seen flames emanate from certain sacred relics, he was not surprised when a ball of lightning rolled over the top of a religious procession he was leading; he simply proclaimed it another miracle.

"'Look aloft,' cried Starbuck. 'The corposants! The corposants!' All the yardarms were tipped with a pallid fire; and touched at each tripointed lightning rod end with those tapering white flames, each of the three tall masts was silently burning in that sulphurous air, like three gigantic wax tapers before the altar."

That's how Melville described Saint Elmo's fire, also known as "corposants," from the Italian *corpo santo*, meaning "holy body" – those sudden fires that appear on yardarms, at the tips of wooden masts, between the horns of cattle, at the tips of airplane wings, and around metal objects, especially at high altitudes.

Saint Elmo's fire was named for a fourth-century Italian bishop who was rescued from drowning by a sailor and ever afterward swore to give a warning of approaching storms to sailors at sea. But in fact, by the time Saint Elmo's fire appears, one is in the midst of a storm – too late to do anything about it.

In the journal of his second voyage, Columbus noted: "On Saturday, at night, the body of St. Elmo was seen, with seven lighted candles in the round top and there followed mighty rain and frightful thunder. I mean the lights were seen which the seamen affirm to be the body of St. Elmo, and they sang litanies and prayers to him, looking upon it as the most certain that in these storms when he appears, there can be no danger."

This "holy body" is actually the swarmlike glow of atmospheric electricity, too low a discharge to be harmful, but high enough to light up the highest points around. Sometimes masses of flying insects carry this incandescent charge and are mistaken for UFOs.

Transient luminous phenomena, like the transient coronary spasms I now experience – little cramps in the heart muscle – have been observed by unmanned spacecraft in the atmospheres of Jupiter, Venus, Saturn, and Uranus, whose cloud layers, made of ammonia ice and filled with particles of water, are spawning grounds for lightning. Do they have afternoon thunderstorms on Jupiter? Does Jupiter have afternoons at all?

Storm-related electrical discharges are shrouded in mystery. No one theory of cloud electrification can account for the prodigious amount of current produced in a thunderstorm. Being in the right place at the right time to get samples – as I was – is not an experiment for which you volunteer.

Gretel Ehrlich was born and raised in California and lives there now. She began to write in 1979 after going to Wyoming as a documentary filmmaker. She also worked on a sheep ranch. Her prose pieces have appeared in The New York Times, The Atlantic, Harper's, *and* New Age Journal. *She has published two books of poetry, a story collection called* City Tales *(with Edward Hoagland) and* Wyoming Stories, *a collection of essays entitled* Islands, Universe, Home. *Also, published by Penguin Books,* The Solace of Open Spaces, *and* A Match to the Heart, *an account of her experience after being struck by lightning. Gretel Ehrlich has received awards from the National Endowment for the Arts and the Wyoming Council of the Arts.*

Jeff Grabmeier

WHEN I WAS FOUR YEARS OLD, a monstrous tornado rumbled through my neighborhood and blew away my house. Eight years later, I decided I wasn't going to be a victim again – so I took up weather forecasting.

It didn't matter that there were trained meteorologists with advanced degrees and sophisticated equipment to do that for me. My experience with the twister proved to me that meteorologists were no better at predicting the weather than I was at predicting the changing moods of my younger brother.

After I begged my parents for a few weeks, they broke down and bought me a weather kit. It was a Mr. Wizard type of setup with a rain collector, wind-speed gauge, barometer, thermometer, and a booklet on forecasting. The instruments were made of flimsy plastic and the book made forecasting seem as easy as getting candy from Grandma, but I couldn't have been happier if Dad had given me a genuine National Weather Service Laboratory. I felt powerful. In control.

I pored over the kit's forecasting book for the next few days. It was exciting to learn about the different cloud formations and the specialized meteorological terms. Soon I was dropping terms like "occluded front" and "temperature inversion" into my everyday conversation.

After a week of intensive study, I was sure I had what it took to forecast the weather. So I set up the equipment in the backyard and launched my new career. I took the job seriously; I'd even leave the outfield in the seventh inning of my Little League game and run home to check the instruments.

Twice each day, I carefully recorded in a small notebook the barometric pressure, wind speed and direction, cloud formations, rainfall, and current conditions. The book taught me what to look for: things like high, wispy cirrus clouds that are bearers of good weather, or cumulus clouds in the summertime that could quickly develop into thunderheads. Each evening, I hand-printed the forecast for my hometown of Toledo, Ohio. My parents proudly displayed it on the refrigerator door next to my brother's schoolwork.

I kept up my forecasts only for a few months. It wasn't that I was doing a bad job; I was just getting bored. I was tired of forecasting your everyday, run-of-the-mill weather. My fantasy was that one day I would be checking the conditions and suddenly realize that another tornado was going to tear through our neighborhood in minutes. In my daydream, I would run door-to-door alerting my neighbors just in time for them to seek safety. But the only real service I could provide was to warn the neighborhood housewives of rain so they could get their laundry off the clotheslines.

The few exciting times were the occasional summer thunderstorms. I knew that when a tornado was near, the barometric pressure drops dramatically in just minutes. So at the first rumblings of thunder, I raced to my bedroom and sat in front of the barometer, watching closely for signs of coming calamity. But there was no more calamity. If only I would have had my weather kit eight years earlier, I thought to myself. April 11, 1965. The day the infamous Palm Sunday tornado swaggered through my neighborhood like a 200-foot bully, killing 16 and injuring 70. The same day 51 twisters raised hell in the Midwest, taking 256 lives.

That Palm Sunday twister is my first childhood memory. I was four years old and I can recall nothing about our house until the night it was blown apart. My memory begins a little after nine o'clock that night when I was awakened by a terrific boom and then a gathering roar. Later, I would hear the sound described as "the bellowing of a million mad bulls." I didn't know anything about bulls, but to me it sounded like the roar of the Thing that occasionally haunted my dreams. All kids have their own personal dream monsters, but my Thing was a 100-foot version of Godzilla, with rows of teeth and scaly green skin.

Mom and Dad were sitting in the kitchen when they heard the clamor. My father opened the back door and saw, etched by the near-constant lightning, the mad dance of the twister. I was sitting on the edge of my bed, confused and scared, when my parents rushed in and grabbed my brother and me. Just as Mom grabbed my one-year-old brother, the window above his crib shattered.

We didn't have a basement, so Mom and Dad headed for a door in the floor of the garage that led to a tiny crawlspace under the house. They ran down the pitch-black hallway. It was as if the Thing was chasing us and we were trying to escape; our legs felt like they were made of lead. Suddenly, the Thing was hovering over us, ripping apart the house. Dad fell on top of me, and Mom on my brother. Everything we owned whirled around us as if controlled by poltergeists. I closed my eyes, protected underneath my father, and wondered what would happen when it caught us. But as quickly as it came, it was gone.

As the roar faded, we stood up in silence. Surprisingly, none of us had suffered anything more severe than scratches and bruises. We looked up from the rubble that had been our home and into the turbulent sky. Our roof was gone. But we still had part of a roof – it belonged to a neighbor and now lay crumpled in our living room. In my bedroom, an asphalt shingle had been hurled with such force that it was embedded in a wooden closet door. We walked aimlessly around the debris like we were waiting for the No. 10 bus.

A few days after the tornado, we moved into a mobile home in our backyard while workers cleaned up the rubble and built a new home on the foundation of the old. Each time a storm passed, I gazed out my bedroom window in the trailer and nervously eyed what was left of my old house. I thought a lot more about the weather than most four-year-olds, trying to make sense of what happened to me. At that young age, I dealt with my fear on a superstitious level. I continued to think of the weather as malevolent, unpredictable, mysterious, and unknowable. I wanted to know how I could trust a world where even a cloud could get to me.

As I grew older and went to school I began to realize that the best way to overcome superstition was with knowledge. That's why I think I wanted that weather kit and why I read so much about meteorology. To an extent, it worked. I felt somewhat better when I learned about the hot and cold air masses and all the other forces that caused tornadoes. But other things I read didn't fit the neat scientific theories – or at least I thought they didn't. The freakish wonders caused by tornadoes and the almost deliberate way they spared some lucky souls seemed to fit more with my old superstitious views of the weather than with my developing scientific ones.

I once read about a twister that hit St. Louis in 1896 which thrust a pine two-by-four through a solid iron wall five-eighths of an inch thick. I knew that tornadoes could produce winds of up to 300 miles per hour, but such a terrific feat still sent shivers up my spine.

Twisters sometimes seem to consciously spare people who by all odds should have been injured or killed. A family in Madison, Indiana, sought shelter in a bedroom closet when a tornado struck April 3, 1974. Every part of their house was knocked to the ground – except the closet in which they hid.

Tornadoes seem to have highly developed senses of humor, too. During a twister in El Dorado, Kansas on June 10, 1958, a woman was blown through a window and carried 60 feet. When she landed, she found a broken copy of the record "Stormy Weather" next to her.

Real scientists might scoff, but to me it seemed tornadoes were playing pranks on the solid, immutable laws of nature. Tornadoes that destroyed houses and left closets standing, threw people in the air and gently set them down, and hurled objects through steel walls seemed more like malevolent demons than meteorological phenomena.

When I started studying tornadoes, I had no idea that praying for the weekend and staying out of cars might be ways of protecting myself. But one scientific study seemed to suggest just that. Researchers found that significantly fewer tornadoes occurred on the weekend than on weekdays. They speculated that auto traffic created little vortexes that, added together, could help account for some tornadoes. That knowledge didn't help ease my fears. If that were true, I felt I might as well just make offerings to Aeolus, the Greek god of wind, rather than take heed in science.

By this time, I was too old to believe in the Thing. And science didn't seem to offer the explanations I craved. But this Aeolus guy had a long history in literature, so maybe it was he who visited me one summer day when I was 17 years old.

It happened when I was sailing an 18-foot sailboat with my father and brother out on Maumee Bay, on the west end of Lake Erie. In the west, black clouds appeared and then quickly covered the sky as if they had foamed over a boiling pot. My father quickly headed the boat toward shore but within minutes Aeolus had blown the bay into a frothy white frenzy. All around us, sailboats capsized in the strong winds.

We soon gave up any hope of reaching the mainland and my father headed the boat for a small island about a half-mile away. But we knew that we had to drop the sails or we would capsize, too. With no other choice, my father gave the helm to my brother and told him to steer toward the island. Dad left the safety of the cockpit and crawled onto the front deck to take down the smaller of the two sails. But he slipped on the rain-slicked deck and fell into the churning water. Luckily, as he fell, he managed to grab onto the forestay of the boat.

Meanwhile, I struggled to release the cable that held up the large mainsail. After a pitched battle with Aeolus, I finally pulled the cable free and the sail dropped. The boat slowed and we drifted to shore.

After this second close call with the weather, I began to wonder how many lives I had and how many Mother Nature was going to take away. For all I had learned, I still hadn't found a way to protect myself from the weather. And I still hadn't found a fail-safe way to know exactly what the weather was going to do.

In many ways, my search was just a variation of one undertaken by many 19th-century scientists, who hoped to find a set of scientific principles that would allow them to predict everything that was going to happen in the universe. That possibility was dashed in 1926 when a German scientist came up with the Uncertainty Principle. The principle states that we can predict future events exactly only if we can perfectly measure the present state of the universe. But the universe has an unpredictable, random element that makes perfect measurement and prediction impossible.

The weather takes the Uncertainty Principle and dumps it on us like a surprise six-inch snowfall. Weather constantly reminds us that we are subject to random forces beyond our control. We are reminded that the universe was born in chaos and will end that way – billions of years from now, we hope.

Even our primitive ancestors understood the connection between weather and chaos. The Apache Indians believed that before the world was created, there existed only Darkness, Water, and Cyclone. For an Apache, seeing a tornado must have been like seeing the world before the dawn of creation. I know how they felt.

When the tornado hit my house, I had my own glimpse of the Earth as it was millions of years ago, when life existed only in a primordial soup. I can imagine mountains thrusting violently from the surface, seas boiling from the heat of the earth and great storms raging across a desolate, empty landscape. Sometimes I can imagine chaos on an even grander scale: Black holes sucking all nearby matter, even light, into their cores. Stars bursting into supernovas and spewing debris that will someday form new planets and new suns.

Nothing seems simple anymore, or even possible to understand. But despite all that is random and unpredictable, I still haven't lost the yearning of that 12-year-old kid with a weather kit. Something keeps me looking for order in my own little corner of the universe.

Jeff Grabmeier is the Assistant Director of Science Communications at Ohio State University. He has written health articles and humorous essays for several Ohio and national magazines.

April is the cruelest month — T.S. Eliot

ONLY A STORM

Robert Henson

SOME PEOPLE, it seems, manage to take tornadoes in stride. There is a videotape, famous among the storm-obsessed, that documents one of the most vicious twisters ever observed in North America. On the tape, you see a dark grey cone tossing objects just over a line of homes near Hesston, Kansas. It is March and the trees of this prairie town, still brown and spindly with late winter, seem unfazed by the funnel a few blocks behind them. As the twister churns along the horizon, the narrator, apparently an older man, slowly and calmly intones, "It's a tornado in Hesston ... going right up the west part of town ... right up Main Street ... right up through the business district ..." No quavering, no helium-high pitch, no heavy breathing ... only a flat recital of the facts.

I can't do this. The air in motion is too visceral, too sensual, for me to be so dispassionate. When the clouds and the wind are tumbling, diving, swooping, I'm right in there with them, feeling every swirl in my gut.

2:00 a.m., April 30, 1970, Oklahoma City. I'm huddled upstairs in the corner of my parents' bedroom, my ten-year-old face pressed to the window. The house is tuned to the storm; it reverberates after each blinding flash. I half expect bricks to start flying off the walls. I try in vain to get a weather report on my parents' clock radio, but all I hear is a mass of static. I can't see anything out the window, beyond the tall houses and wind-tossed trees, except rain and darkness.

Only my father is home tonight. When I hear the wail of the sirens, I jostle my sleeping dad. He rolls over and mumbles, "There aren't any tornadoes. Don't worry." I worry anyway. It feels like my role, my duty. If my hyperawareness can't ward off the storm, nothing can.

There is no avoiding storms when you grow up in Oklahoma. Like the smell of hay and the native twang, they are part of the fabric of life and they command your attention like nothing else. Some Oklahomans regard storms as one might regard mosquitos, irritating pests from which no baseball game or senior picnic is safe. Others enjoy them as lighthearted diversions, curious if not compelling, just another wacky feature of life on the Great Plains. Most folks, though, are storm-hardened and proud of it, watching the annual convection parade with both fondness and fear.

For me, the sculpted thunderheads embodied all that was majestic, powerful, and uncertain about life. The yellow, faded "FALLOUT SHELTER" stickers on the stairwells at my school had a vague creepiness to them, but they were abstract, a relic of danger from another place and time. I couldn't put tornadoes on the shelf so easily. How could I sleep on a stormy night knowing that the house might disintegrate around us?

After what must have been an hour of white flashes and ear-splitting crashes, the storm's volume begins to ratchet down. I start to relax. Maybe Dad's right.

The next day, in my fifth-grade classroom, rumors fly about a tornado having hit town. When I get home and spread out the evening's Oklahoma City Times, *there it is, laid out for me in black and white with a headline as big as World War III: TWISTER RIPS THROUGH CITY. Nobody had died, but 50 people were hurt and dozens of homes and businesses had been destroyed between 2:00 and 3:00 a.m. The path was less than four miles from my house.*

During my childhood, I was rooted to the earth as I watched the familiar phases of each storm pass by. The show would begin with lacy, gilt-edged sheets of cirrus sweeping in from the west. These would soon be flanked by coarse rolls of gunmetal-gray arcus clouds and the first intimations of thunder. Before long came a symphonic torrent of rain and ice, punctuated by split seconds where the universe seemed to crack into jagged pieces of light and sound. Finally, after the decrescendo, came the deep-breathed aftermath, where the sunlight was clean and even the mundane swoosh of cars driving through waterlogged roads sounded musical.

I'd watch it all unfold from the window or the side porch, unable to do or think about anything else. As terrified as I was of what the storm might bring, I was also intensely curious. How could the atmosphere take water vapor and use it to create so many kinds of clouds? So many shadings of wind and light and water, so much drama?

Yet no matter how violent the hail or insistent the wind, every storm of my childhood ended with an anticlimax. Never did I see the sinuous, ominous curve of a funnel over the rooftops of our neighborhood. Each mournful siren blast was followed sooner or later by its counterpart, the all-clear signal.

I watched and wondered. Would my family ever find ourselves pawing our way through bricks and timber after the all-clear? Might we ever emerge from our basement into a leveled world? Buried in the midst of my swirling fear of storms, there lay a nugget of strange hope. I'd picture our family starting from scratch, all our problems and worries blown away by the same twister I'd dreaded for so long. We'd have passed through the belly of the beast and survived. My curiosity would be satisfied and, somehow, my fear would be gone.

On those spring nights of my childhood when it seemed disaster was breathing down our necks, we huddled in the basement between piles of laundry. I'd pace back and forth, window-deprived and edgy. My brothers and sisters would tell jokes. Dad would stand and smoke, faintly embarrassed to be taking shelter. Mom would sit on the washing machine and rally us. If I seemed especially tense, she'd tell me in a low, soothing voice, "You know, you'll never be a meteorologist if you're afraid of storms." Could she have anticipated that a few years later, I'd be chasing them?

It was the spring of 1981 and I was a wide-eyed undergraduate, driving the back roads of Oklahoma in search of my first tornado. For the first time, I was maneuvering around storms that seemed to have leapt out of my meteorology textbooks. I'd study the clouds from different angles, fill in gaps in my knowledge, all the while joined by others as passionate about storms as I was.

During the school year, I attended Rice University, mired in the swamps of Houston, where the storms felt half-hearted and incomplete to me. The softest-looking cumulus cloud would dump truckloads of rain, spit out some lightning, and float along its way. By spring I was longing for the semester's end, when I could return to Oklahoma and be reunited with storms that meant business.

On one fine May day, the sky full of bubbling cumulus, I headed west from Oklahoma City on Interstate 40 with Mike and Randy, two of the world's few experienced storm chasers at that time. It was Sunday morning, and as Mike and Randy bantered and traded jargon, I felt like a newcomer to the temple. Eight hours, 300 miles, and innumerable turns later, we found ourselves in the northeast corner of Oklahoma with a fellow carload of chasers, watching a field of churning grey cloud above us. Suddenly someone from the other car pointed to the southwest and yelled "Tornado on the ground! Tornado on the ground!" I had only a second's glimpse of the ropy funnel, no more than a mile or so away, before we scooted to safety. As darkness swept in, the storm passed to our north, where lightning flashed with the staccato rhythms of Morse code, pulse after pulse crashing to earth. During a few flashes I caught a glimpse of a cone-shaped lowering on the horizon. On the long drive back to Norman, the reality seeped in: I had finally seen a tornado.

I remained terrified of twisters after that day, but my uncertain soul kept me going on the road, following storm after storm, taking pictures and taking notes, coming to terms with the demons that had prowled across my childhood.

Three years later, I came to the University of Oklahoma for graduate school and stepped up my storm chasing. It was the mid-1980s, still light years before the film *Twister*. Chasing was art as much as science, carried out by a motley group with CB radios, hand-drawn weather maps, and beat-up sedans. I leapt in wholeheartedly, itching for each round of storms to give me a purpose and shake my spirit.

The dangers in the sky were clear enough to me, but the dangers of the road didn't mean as much until my first spring of graduate school. One evening, a particularly vicious squall line tore across the state. I returned from an exciting, satisfying chase to the meteorology department late that night. A fellow grad student met us at the department door with a gray, blank stare, and I soon learned that an undergraduate from the department had just died. Like me, Chris had been pursuing storms that afternoon. He'd spun out of control on a dirt road while trying to avoid an animal. After the wreck, I was told, Chris had stepped out of his car, paused for a moment, and then quietly collapsed from internal injuries.

On many spring evenings of my childhood, after dinner was over and the sitcoms had started, I'd settle in to watch TV. In ten or twenty minutes, the show would be interrupted by a beep-beep-beep and the words "WEATHER ADVISORY" superimposed on a hand-drawn cloud. Then my childhood idol, weathercaster Jim Williams – sporting hip sideburns and gifted with a honey-rich Oklahoma drawl – would come onscreen in front of a state map. There'd be a rectangle drawn in chalk somewhere across the state's western reaches, with the words "TORNADO WATCH" written above.

For the next few hours, I knew I'd be trotting back and forth between the TV set and the window. I'd feel the threads of my gut tighten. I'd sense my mind half-wanting and half-dreading the tempest to come. My lifeline was the TV set and the calm, warm, authoritative tone of Jim Williams. He seemed so knowledgeable, and yet I knew, in a child's sober way of knowing things, that he, like the rest of us, would be utterly vulnerable before an onslaught of 300-mile-an-hour wind. How could Jim Williams not be as afraid as I was? In ten or twenty years, would knowledge be able to ease my mind, too, as it seemed to ease his?

I didn't stop chasing after Chris died, although a better part of me felt I should. The act became a guilty pleasure, laced with a new acknowledgment of risk. The panorama of sky and cloud remained every bit as compelling, but more and more I felt numbed by the hundreds of miles spent driving through sheets of rain, the backtracking and detouring, the bluster and bravado among those of us denying the threats we faced and the pain that our much-loved storms brought to others.

There was still plenty to learn, though. I spent my first summer after grad school in Colorado, part of a team of eight chasers taking photos and videos of severe storms. Our findings were compared to returns from an experimental Doppler radar (the kind now deployed across the country) to learn what the bright colors and complex patterns were telling us about the real world of storms.

These High Plains storms, I found, were as different from Oklahoma supercells as a wet Massachusetts snow is from Colorado's champagne powder. Violent tornadoes were almost unheard of here. Instead, the clean, high air nourished landspouts, the terrestrial equivalent of waterspouts. They often formed and died in minutes, sporting a narrow funnel at the top, a dust cloud below, and a transparent midsection. In the thinner, drier air of the High Plains, with virtually no trees or towns to block your view, you could see a landspout from 10 or 20 miles away and a massive hailstorm as far as 100 miles out. It was as if I'd cleaned a pair of dirty eyeglasses and put them back on.

Each day we'd start in Boulder, perched where the High Plains meet the Rockies. We'd drift eastward with the afternoon's storms, which usually grew in size and strength as they moved further from the mountains. Then we'd return to Boulder, typically to a calm, cool summer night. For once, I found myself sleeping in storm season with confidence that a surprise tornado wouldn't – couldn't – steamroll through my home. Instead of being planted in the middle of a meteorological football field, with air masses muscling each other back and forth, I was on the sidelines, watching the show in safety.

I stayed in Boulder and shifted from weather research to writing. Still, these Colorado storms, so clear-eyed and tame next to Oklahoma's, cast their shadows in my life. Each spring, I'd look to the east with bittersweetness. I knew we wouldn't get roof-rattling, middle-of-the-night superstorms here. Like Mohammed, I would have to go to these mountains in the sky in order to feel their power. And chasing brought with it all the baggage that I'd come to know: fatigue, risk, and soul-searching.

One April evening, I dashed to Kansas with a friend to catch what looked to be a smorgasbord of storms the next day. We ended up just east of Wichita minutes before a series of monstrous tornadoes ripped through the area. We caught three of them; the last one turned a ghostly gray as it passed over a lake. The storm itself was breathtaking, a brutally efficient machine twirling through the unending Kansas sky. As we drove northeast to stay with the storm, we noticed hundreds of tiny pink specks descending through the air. In a moment, it dawned on me: this was insulation. We heard later that over a dozen people had been killed in a mobile-home park that was pulverized near Andover.

Later that night, I tossed in my hotel bed, wondering just what it was I had driven 600 miles to see. Was storm chasing really any better than ambulance chasing?

These days I think of myself as a semi-retired chaser. When I see the fronts and the jet stream coming into that certain alignment, my adrenaline still pumps. However, I now have a full life separate from the universe of storms. Now I can gaze out my window at a far-off mound of cumulus, bubbling like popcorn over a stove, and savor its beauty instead of feeling compelled to hop in the car and hunt it down.

On those rare afternoons when I do go out, it's often to see the offbeat storms: the early- or late-season surprises, or the isolated beauty that sits forlornly on the Plains, thumbing its nose at a dry forecast. I'm less likely to encounter hordes of other storm chasers this way, but I'm more likely to find the silent, spiritual locus that I seek. I'll feel the wind hustling toward the storm's core, drawn in by a hurricane-force updraft, and I'll marvel at how mere air can feel so solid. I'll listen for the drumbeat of a hail core a mile or two away. I'll snap a photo of an unearthly deck of mammatus clouds dangling overhead, or a sunlit turret of cumulus beyond the next grain elevator.

Recently I looked at a chaser's Internet page posted only days after a successful chase in Kansas. There it was, a pixelated tornado, frozen in time for the universe to see. I was unmoved. Perhaps I've seen enough in person to know that neither the storm of my dreams nor the tornado of my nightmares has ever really existed. There can be no "perfect storm" for me any more.

Once in a rare while, I'll still find myself face to face with a supercell, the long-lived breed of storms that spawns most killer tornadoes, like the one near Andover, Kansas, on April 26, 1991. There is nothing beautiful about a twister destroying a family's home or taking their lives. How utterly ironic, then, that tornado-producing storms can be the most mesmerizing. The same forces that line up to produce the twister also arrange clouds, wind, and water in spellbinding ways. There is a strange solace in watching such a creation – at once breathtaking and terrible, like life itself.

One can admire a supercell dubiously, as one admires the efficiency of an enormous, well-schooled army or the fluid power of a judo master. There is more to it, though. Each storm has its own character, and its moments of perfection always fray. This is when I have my camera ready, hoping for a bend of refracted light or a stray shred of cloud that can take this storm into the realm of the sublime.

When the sky plays in such wondrous tones, it is hard for me not to listen. Somewhere in the orchestra, I can hear the strains of the universe addressing a small, scared child, telling him there is as much to admire as there is to fear in the workings of this paradoxical planet. It's a message I can never hear too many times.

Robert Henson, a native of Oklahoma City, has lived in Boulder, Colorado, since 1987. He is a writer/editor at the University Corporation for Atmospheric Research and has written for Discover, American Scientist, Sierra, *and other magazines. A contributing editor of* Weatherwise *magazine, Henson is also a frequent contributor to* The Weather Notebook. *After earning an interdisciplinary bachelor's degree in meteorology at Rice University, Henson completed extensive graduate work at the University of Oklahoma's esteemed meteorology school before earning a master's degree from OU in journalism. He enjoys biking, hiking, and marveling at the workings of the atmosphere.*

Within Mount Washington Clouds

Robert Irion

CALIFORNIA IS FULL of transplanted Vermonters, like me. We move here for school or work, and the wiles of the West Coast conspire to keep us. Whenever two of us meet, we dispense with the secret Vermont handshake to reminisce about what we left behind for the earthquakes, mudslides, and wildfires of our adopted state. Real maple syrup is high on the list, as are cross-country skiing, autumn foliage, and (sadly) the Red Sox. But I'm the only one, it seems, who misses another joy that New England offers: clouds.

Here on California's central coast, we don't get much in the way of clouds. Dense fog advances and recedes during summer months, draping the shoreline and the redwoods of coastal foothills. The fog unveils a warm and trustworthy blue sky, but it does little to stir the soul. Winter brings a monotonous succession of storms from the Pacific, so laden with moisture that a dull gray dome clamps the heavens. "Not all clouds are interesting or exciting," wrote photographer Ralph Steiner in his 1985 book, *In Pursuit of Clouds*. He might well have had California in mind.

Steiner knew where to live: Vermont, which enriched my childhood with ever-changing clouds. I would interpret the Rorschach skies during evening walks with my dog along a road that overlooked Lake Champlain and the Adirondacks of northern New York. I loved sunsets over the lake, the play of light within feathery cirrus, and the bulging cumulus clouds that loomed darkly. Approaching storm fronts were a particular thrill; more than once I ran home as a sharp line of showers raced across the fields. The rain usually won.

But it wasn't until after I went to the Massachusetts Institute of Technology that I appreciated clouds as more than fanciful "demons of the air," as people in the dark ages called them. The first part of this change was purely intellectual. During my studies in planetary science, I learned of Earth's hydrologic cycle, the ceaseless rhythm of evaporation and condensation that drives the flow of water among land, sea, and sky. The scale of this cycle startled me; I was amazed that 3.5 billion gallons of water falls to the globe's surface every second, on average. Soon, clouds were no longer just evocative fluffballs, but visual clues to the atmosphere's complex churnings. I learned to read their messages, and I realized those old weather rhymes were little nuggets of science in sailor's code. "Mackerel scales and mares' tails / make lofty ships carry low sails," for instance, means that a sky full of cirrocumulus clouds portends rain within a day. I wasn't planning to become a meteorologist, but I enjoyed looking skyward with more than simple wonder.

The second part of my transformation, some two years after my graduation, was richer than the pages of a text could provide. It involved a hike into the clouds themselves, at a special place with a central figure in my life, and at a time when I was ready to see the world with eyes unfettered from the petulance of an earlier age. That experience had its roots not in my own youth but in my father's, a generation before I was born.

Most of us have one place that we treasure above all others. This place holds deep sentimental value, renewed through the years by occasional visits or glances through a well-worn photo album. A childhood home, a tiny wedding chapel, the field where a Little League championship was won – such are the places that time preserves and crystallizes, rather than erodes, in our minds. For my father, that place is Mount Washington.

He first scaled the 6,288-foot peak in northern New Hampshire in 1946 as a limber 21-year-old fresh from his Army tour in Europe. Many times since, he returned to ski the mountain's fierce slopes or take family and friends up through the spectacular bowl of Tuckerman Ravine to the boulder-strewn summit. While Mount Washington may seem a pimple next to the peaks of the Rocky Mountains or the Sierra Nevada, it reigns supreme in the eastern United States. It's also the site of the country's most unpredictable weather, a fact that usually prefaced my father's tales of his adventures there.

I joined my father on his last two ascents of Mount Washington. The first time, I was just 16 and at the zenith of what I suppose was my normal teenage rebellious phase. I had quit the Boy Scouts some years before and was irritated that I once again had to camp and eat from dried-food packets, although I recall a grudging admiration at my father's skill in packing things and preparing for all conceivable weather. I felt safe, and reaching the top was a rush. However, my father, who was then 55, barely made it. On the long way down, it seemed his knees would fail utterly. I moped and muttered, oblivious to both rocks and sky.

It thus came as some surprise when he proposed a return to Mount Washington seven summers later, just before I was to move across the continent. My mother and I were dubious, but I sensed his resolve. Today, I wonder whether he sensed something in me as well, that the journey would be more rewarding because I had fledged the nest. Whatever his motivation, I consented, provided that we attempt the ascent and descent in one day (I still wasn't in the mood to camp). We met at a motel near Pinkham Notch, the starting point of our hike, to prepare for our 7 A.M. departure.

The skies dawned partly sunny, but the afternoon forecast for the top of the mountain predicted thick clouds, possible showers, and winds gusting near 50 miles per hour. That was typical, we knew. Mount Washington and the rest of New Hampshire's White Mountains present a hurdle to the air that sweeps across New England, forcing it upward in a process called "orographic lifting." This does two things. First, it accelerates the air flow to speeds that routinely exceed gale force. Second, the air cools rapidly as it climbs, until its water vapor condenses into clouds that cocoon the summit five days out of six. We would become intimately familiar with cloud origins later in the day, but at the outset we felt undeterred by the tame threat of "possible showers."

The hike is a rigorous 4.1-mile climb, the first 2.4 miles of which meanders through the woods between Pinkham Notch and Tuckerman Ravine. The trail gets gradually steeper here but is fairly boring; views of the sky are confined to narrow lanes between branches. As we walked, the humidity in the air and the sweat on my back made me recall a delightful book I had unearthed at MIT, a 1926 volume titled *Fogs and Clouds* by meteorologist W. J. Humphreys of the U.S. Weather Bureau. Water evaporates slowly (and skin sweats profusely) on such days, Humphreys noted, because the air already holds so much moisture. His point was memorable, for he made it in this way: "The wash on the clothesline, as every housewife knows, dries provokingly slowly during cloudy, muggy weather." Modern editors might not look kindly upon such an observation, I mused.

The real fun of the hike begins at Tuckerman Ravine, a huge double bowl carved by glaciers millions of years ago. In the winter, Tuckerman fills with snow. Daring skiers plunge over the lip of the "headwall," the nearly vertical face at the top of Tuckerman, to fly at breakneck speeds between jagged outcrops of rock. The mountain frames Tuckerman with Boott Spur and Lion's Head, two massive shoulders that provide more challenging climbs for the less faint of heart or body.

Pockets of snow remain in Tuckerman year-round, but in the summer the ravine is speckled by hikers drawn to the beauty of the place. Water endlessly cascades over the headwall, gathering strength from countless rivulets to form a narrow but lovely waterfall in the center of the ravine. The white of the snow is displaced by the green of grasses, the grays and tans of ancient rock, and the subtle whites and yellows of wildflowers.

As my father and I slowly ascended past the first bowl and into the smaller, steeper second cirque, we were lulled by the natural quiet of the place, the constant sounds of wind and water and nothing else. An occasional hiker hailed us and encouraged us onward; otherwise, we were alone under the graying sky, undisturbed even by bird or insect.

I pointed out to my father that we faced a damp road ahead. Small hooks of mist, called "virga," dangled from the bases of the clouds that gathered above the headwall like sentinels, daring us to pass. This meant the tiny water particles within the clouds had coalesced enough to begin to fall, but they couldn't quite reach the ground before evaporating. I wasn't worried about lightning or a squall, since I'd seen no signs of the fantastically high cumulus clouds that signify a really unstable atmosphere. However, it did mean we would enter what amounted to a fog bank. As hot as we were at the moment, that sounded enticing.

Memories surfaced like tiny seeds as we climbed, flowering briefly at rest stops before being replanted for future nourishment.

*Right about here is where your mother and I hiked to in 1949, the year after we were married. It was raining and the rocks were slippery; we must have been the only people in the whole ravine. She hated it, she couldn't believe people would actually **want** to come here. We finally turned back.*

A man passed us with his two golden retrievers as we rested near the last patch of snow at the waterfall's base. One of them bounded up the rocks with seemingly limitless energy, but the other straggled behind, its tongue lolling not with drippy canine enthusiasm but with fatigue.

Later, the man passed us again, this time on his way down as we were inching nearer the summit. Only the first dog was with him; the second, we learned, was being taken down by a ranger, its back legs lamed by the ascent.

I wondered what dogs think of this silly mountain-climbing fondness we humans have. They can't appreciate views.

Over there, Rob, I skied down the headwall. Just once. We had to climb straight up the wall on narrow steps gouged into the snow, then strap on our skis at the top. There was barely room to turn around, then ZOOM! I was off. I felt like my legs were out of control.

Were you scared?

Yes.

Our rest stops became more frequent as we neared the crest of the headwall. Finally, at noon, we reached the famous sign at the top of the wall that marks the junction of several hiking trails. One trail continued to the summit, a half-mile away.

STOP, the sign reads. THE AREA AHEAD HAS THE WORST WEATHER IN AMERICA. MANY HAVE DIED THERE FROM EXPOSURE, EVEN IN THE SUMMER. TURN BACK NOW IF THE WEATHER IS BAD.

We looked at the summit. It was shrouded in clouds, gray patches scudding across the craggy face of the mountain. The wind where we stood already was strong enough to knock us off balance. So, of course, we did the only proper thing: we pressed on.

Seven years ago, do you remember? We hiked to here in the afternoon, but we left our gear below because we weren't going to go for the summit until the next day. Then a storm hit. You decided we should go straight instead of turning back, that we should try to make it to the Lake of the Clouds hut, a mile away. There was lightning in the air, the wind was howling, we got soaked. I fell on the rocks. Like any kid would, I acted like I was miserable. But I was exhilarated.

This part of the mountain is no more than a vast pile of boulders, with the trail marked by yellow paint and cairns of rock. The wind got stronger as we clambered into the lowering veil we'd seen from Tuckerman. The knowledge that I was now inside a cloud, that I was breathing a cloud whipping past the mountain, was incredible. "I love this!" I shouted.

But as my father's breathing grew more labored, I knew we'd need to take our time. I was patient, certainly more patient than I had been seven years before. I waited, walked, waited. Engulfed by the cloud, I began to think. My senses, so shuttered at age 16 but keenly aware now, drew connections between my studies in high-priced classrooms and the real world near 6,000 feet.

In his book, Humphreys wrote: "Fog is a cloud on the Earth; cloud, a fog in the sky." It struck me as a matter of semantics. Yes, we were still on the ground, and thus within a "fog." Yet a distant observer would see the top of Mount Washington vanish into a blanket of nimbostratus clouds. So, cloud it was, in my mind.

Could I begin to grasp the tenuousness of clouds, even the thickest ones? The ones that, on idle summer days, floated overhead like inviting pillows? Sweeping my hands ahead of me, I envisioned an experiment to measure the water content of a volume of cloud. Humphreys described just such a test, conducted in a dense fog off the coast of Newfoundland aboard a Coast Guard ship in 1915. By using a hot wire grating to evaporate all the droplets within a volume of air, scientists determined that a block of fog three feet wide, six feet high, and 100 feet long (the limit of their visibility) held one-seventh of a glass of water, distributed among 60 billion drops. "Barely one good swallow!" Humphreys exclaimed. I reasoned that my canteen, half empty as it was, might fill Tuckerman Ravine with cloud if I could pulverize the water to trillions of teensy bits, each one just a hundredth of a millimeter across.

As I felt the cool cloud in my throat, I recognized that I was inhaling more than just water. When it reaches the right temperature and humidity to condense, water vapor needs some "nucleus" to start a droplet. Dust from the ground does the trick, as does sea salt, pollen, spores, soot from smokestacks or forest fires, volcanic ash, jet exhaust, and even the vaporized remains of micrometeorites that constantly bombard Earth. So many more of these particles waft above continents than above the ocean that a cloud over land has a harder time forming rain or snow. If too many nuclei fight for the available moisture, the droplets may stay too small to fall out of the cloud.

Above us, near the summit, a hiker with a good set of lungs launched into an aria from some opera or another. The notes blew down to us, distorted, and the feeling that I was in a different world only grew.

We rested a last time, smiling and sodden. No views would await us, but in my altered state that didn't seem to matter. I closed my eyes as my father shared a final memory.

Your sister Susan and I hiked Lion's Head when she was just 7. I had to help her climb some of the bigger boulders. She was frightened in the fog, but I kept talking to her and coaxing her toward my voice. Then the fog cleared, and we saw the most glorious sunset. Golds and the deepest pinks I've ever seen. I still remember what she said: "It's like we're in heaven."

I could come back here again and again.

The top was finally visible through the thickening gloom, in the form of the front of a pickup truck poking over the edge of the parking lot. Tourists would crowd the top, waiting in the cafeteria for the miserable weather to lift before driving back down the mountain. Our ascent within Mount Washington clouds, I thought, deserved a more primeval end.

I climbed over the last few boulders and reached the summit, walking in my father's footsteps.

Robert Irion grew up in rural Vermont and still visits New England whenever he can. He received a B.S. in Earth and Planetary Sciences from Massachusetts Institute of Technology and a certificate in Science Communication from the University of California, Santa Cruz. He now writes about research in the physical sciences for Astronomy, New Scientist, Science, *and other magazines. He lives in Santa Cruz, California.*

SUNDAYS IN THE SKY

John Hanson Mitchell

FROM THE MEADOW in which I am now lying, I can see a mere slice of sky between the surrounding trees. It is clear, warm, also September, and a northwest wind is ringing down high, fair-weather clouds that sail down the ridge like tall ships and cross above me. A late night has sapped me of all ambition, so instead of working in the garden as I had intended, I lie on my back in the grass to rest a while, perhaps to sleep. But there is too much happening.

A few yards above me, green darner butterflies dart by, the meadow crickets are singing madly in the surrounding fields, and the little red dragonflies in the genus *Sympetrum* land here and there beside me, zoom off on a mission, and then return to land. I alternately doze and wake and watch the sky.

I am staring into an ill-defined, infinite atmosphere, a space of nothingness where the air is bell clear. But, in the space of a few minutes, things float, wing, drift, or fly by: a broad-winged hawk, crows, something dark and fast (probably a dragonfly), a slow-flying wasp, its legs dangling, more fluff, and ever and always the great parade of clouds.

Hamlet saw camels in the clouds, then weasels, then a whale. The English painter John Constable saw brooding landscapes, Fragonard saw porcelain, Turner saw fire and conflagration. The illustrator N. C. Wyeth, the father of Andrew, saw a great sky giant passing in the thunderheads beyond the shores of the Atlantic beaches. All I see today is a dog's head, first a spaniel, blunt nosed, with a rounded forehead, then something with a longer nose, then something very much like a Doberman. Or was I dreaming?

Just as the Doberman's head breaks up, I see tiny specks against the white cloud. I know better than to let specks drift by on a September day, so I rouse myself, go into the house, and return with binoculars. There, overhead, descending now in a long stretched-out line, are ten or twenty hawks, probably broadwings, drifting out of a gyre. I doze again.

Crows call. I open an eye and watch a flight shift from the white pines on top of the ridge to the hickories on the southeastern slope. Much excitement among them. much cawing, with bowed heads and beaks. A red balloon, high amidst the blue, slowly proceeds to the southeast, as if on a mission. A plane drones by, headed west, then another, also headed west. One follows a few minutes later, a type known, I believe, as a Tomahawk. (Why do so many small planes and fast cars have to be named for weapons or predatory birds and mammals? I wonder.)

I used to have a problem with low-flying, noisy planes passing over the meadow on Sunday mornings. I made inquiries and found that in all likelihood, it was the work of weekend pilots, flying out to breakfast at various airports west of Boston. After the Tomahawk passes, I try to make a calculation of the amount of energy that must be wasted in these breakfast flights, but I fall asleep before I can even begin to figure anything.

A hawk screams, a real one. A red-tail, headed in the wrong direction – northeast. Spiderlings on gossamer drift past, their lines glistening in the sun. Flies skip just above me, a bee, more fluff, another plane, and then high up, its wings steady and its long neck stretched southward, an impossible vision, an anhinga!

I snatch up the binoculars and look more carefully and have to conclude that this is an exceptionally long-necked cormorant. I fall back. Ten minutes later, a flight of some ten to fifteen cormorants drifts by, high against the steady march of clouds.

I am used to these surprises in the sky. Once, lying in this same meadow on a summer evening, watching the bats course overhead, I saw an immense tropical bat materialize out from the dark wall of trees beyond the clearing. It soared above me in a twisting flight, dove, and rose again, and, by the time I realized it was a nighthawk, it was gone.

After lunch I fall into a deep sleep. By midafternoon the great parade is still passing – the hawks, the dragons, the fluff, the slow procession of shiplike clouds. It strikes me that elsewhere in the world this must be one of those autumnal days when watchers of the skies see massive flights of hawks passing down the ridges, so, refreshed from my nap, I drive to a nearby cleared height and spend an hour watching the western sky. Nothing appears, the winds have dropped, the clouds settle into low-lying banks in the west, like distant dunes. I should have stayed home.

That night after dark I went back to the meadow. The fair-weather clouds had dispersed, and the black sky was moonless and clear. Overhead I could see the last of the Summer Triangle, with the great constellation, the Swan, at one angle. Like all good migratory birds, now that autumn had arrived, she had swum her long neck around to the south.

Reprinted from Sanctuary Magazine, *Massachusetts Audubon Society. Used by permission of the publisher.*

John Hanson Mitchell is editor of Sanctuary Magazine, *published by the Massachusetts Audubon Society, and author of several books dealing with the natural and human history of a single square mile of land known as Scratch Flat. His latest book,* Trespassing, *is an inquiry into the private ownership of land.*

Un earthing
the SKY

Vast Father Sky —
Dancing to be Rain,
Singing to be Dawn,
Praying to be Night,
And Wed to
Mother Earth.
FROM SPIRIT-EARTH SERIES

Paul M. Breeden

I GREW UP in a hazy little south Jersey mill town, a place built nearby vast deposits of silica sand, the basic ingredient for making glass. As a kid, I wasn't much of a glass aficionado and didn't care to be a glass expert like my Dad. Nor did I wish to puff my cheeks into duffel bags like my all-time champion grandfather who before him had blown the longest, fattest glass tubing by lungs alone. I was the maverick young artist, already embarked upon the life-long quest for the "perfect sky" and intrigued with what may be found beneath the wild blue yonder.

After all, I was a rock & mineral, butterfly and dead snake collector outdoor boy who felt that good ol' Mother Nature had already beat the heck out of us with primal wildness – her own brand of creativity, evolving miraculous creatures, infinite spaces, colors, textures and forms – a unique type of beauty which, due to its non-synthetic nature, was far, far superior to anything we humans could whip together in a vat. In my mind, if ever there was any true test of quality, the "earthier," the better.

Despite my back-to-earth attitude, and my desire to make paints out of woodsy stuff like the Indians had, I couldn't avoid the lure of "modern" technology. Hey! – my sky was full of streamlined fins, chrome was plastered on every available surface and suddenly, at eight years old, I found myself impossibly perched high atop the fireplug by the street in front of my house, thinking like a mad young scientist that I didn't want to be left behind. Not that it helped relieve my complete distaste for science, math, geography or any kind of school.

Within no time I presented my father with what I felt must be the most unfathomable scientific riddle of all: "How did they ever make the first really straight line?" (like for machines, or a ruler). And you know I felt pretty proud that I had completely stumped my own Dad, this guy who, as a brilliant designer, worked daily with straight edges, rulers, needle-sharp pencils, and the lines of complex design.

With the ultimate scientific mystery unsolved, I headed back out to the nearby woods, the sweet-scented streams and the creepy crawlers of the outdoor world (forget book learnin'), in search of whatever it was. But some geologic prankster had long ago plopped my home town in a pancake-flat world of sand, and the only thing that broke the monotony of it all was a non-stunted tree or some man-made construction. There just weren't any Red River Valleys, cliffs or gold-rich ravines with outcrops of sparkling crystals waiting to quench the fever I had.

By the time I was twelve or so, I began hanging around the gravel plant on the railroad siding at the end of our dead-end street. It was the only place for miles that had anything resembling a hill. So here was my first taste of rarefied altitude, all thirty feet of heaped gravel for a truck ramp. The sloping options were endless: snow sled suicide runs, bicycle crash-testing, a launch pad for my home-made monster kite tossing at the end of a quarter mile of knotted strings. And a place to savor the dusky remnants of a blazing sunset, spying killdeers dog-fighting with the dark; their fluid calls echoing in woods.

One day there, I began noticing the stones beneath my feet, the loose and skittering pebbles of the gravel pile which was my vantage point for the panorama of flat. Already crazed with collector lust, most any unusual shape or texture fanned the flames of my curiosity.

Without a proper rock pick, I couldn't crack open these mundane stones to unleash the potential treasures inside. So I took to spending countless hours practicing my aim by heaving the stones at a nearby steel plate, carefully watching the fragments fly and hoping the shattered home runs wouldn't end up in the weedy outfields.

As soon as the dust settled, I'd scurry up, gather the bits and pieces to quite often be utterly astonished at what had come to light – amazing worm-like extrusions, fossils, geode-crystals, weird sea-bed concretions, until one day I cracked open a little walnut-size stone which was to me, *The Wonder of All Wonders*. Like a Fabergé egg, this unexpected treasure had opened up in neat halves to reveal a secret, hidden fantasy world of wondrous blue. It was as if within the hollow of this dusty brown stone, some wizard had crafted a miniature model of the sky itself – billowing, cloud-like rounds as smooth and sensuous as a summer day. I was simply and totally ecstatic at this find. Nothing, I felt, could ever beat this most uplifting reminder to also keep an eye on the above.

But my interest waned in this private gravel-mining claim and I needed a higher high. Next to the hill was the taboo tower with a nightmarish ladder of endless slippery rungs that reached to the sky itself. What a view! – the whole dreary checkerboard of town, the entire barren wastes of the woods stretched to the distant flat horizon. The breeze rumpled my hair as I fetched unhappy pigeons out of their hideouts there and carted them home for aesthetic modifications. Already the discontented artist, the birds seemed a bit drab to me and thinking they were frayed domestic outcasts from some grimy city, I gently worked prettier markings on their wings with model paints. And then I'd marvel as they set flight in a graceful arc, instantly zeroed in their coordinates and homed right back in to their tower, so confidently and magically navigating in thin, invisible air.

By my teens, delinquent wanderlust led me to the rails leading out of town, my buddy and I stumbling thousands of sweaty steps just to take a swim. Deranged grasshoppers popped like creosoted popcorn from the skillet-hot rail bed cinders, and dazed crows wafted their coal black wings through the oven of the sky. But we'd get there, sustained by hot sodas along the way, and jump into the perfect Olympic pool water of quarried-out sand holes – huge pits dredged of sand for making glass in the furnaces in town.

It was out here in this wasteland of whiteness that they had years before found a sizeable meteorite, probably as simply as picking a penny off a sidewalk. But I never found much more than an arrowhead or some shards of pottery. I never dreamed of finding anything more grand in this bleached badlands of sand.

But one day, climbing the steep, shifting slopes of the sand hole to launch a running dive into the waters below, my ground-scanning habits all paid off! Here was something strangely foreign in the naked sands. My eyes became high-powered fiber-optic electron-microscopic image-fixing radio-telescopic lasers and cancelled out the Tarzan yell and the cannonball dive I had planned.

Here was an oddity the likes of which I'd never seen – sandy on the outside, glassy on the inside. Exactly the same color as the surrounding sands, as if a sticky, hollow worm had gathered clots of grainy annoyance on a trip through the sand. This mysterious scrap, only a couple inches long and a half inch round just riveted me to the spot. I looked for more (swimming could wait), because the ends of this thing did appear to be cleanly broken off, like candy canes without the wrapper. I found more, and then it became clear that these things had come from above, in more ways than one.

Later at home, I showed my amazing finds to my father, and this time he had the answer: It was glass. Oh, but it wasn't just some slippery factory product or a hand-blown knickknack. It was for sure a fulgurite – literally *lightning stone* – formed by lightning striking the sandy ground. Yikes! – this was Big Time rock & mineral stuff! My father, my buddy and I got back to that sand hole as fast as possible, figuring there had to be a big mother lode somewhere in that hill. Shovels aside, we located the main trunk of it by carefully hand-sweeping layers of sand. Ozone-sizzling excitement overtook us all to think that right here, through some slashing torrent a horrendous piercing shock of raw electricity had jolted with all its violence into this very slope and burned a bizarre hole maybe deeper than one could ever imagine, right where we now squatted with shoes full of sand.

We dug for hours, carefully exposing a root-like tunnel of sand-encrusted glass, which branched and twisted like a full-scale model of the jagged-fingered zaps we see in midnight skies. Deeper and deeper we dug, unearthing this "fossil" record of a storm's fury, tracing the arteries of this skeletal apparition which had fused, in the pulsing torment of a split-second inferno, the energy of the basking earth and the power of the rampaging sky.

Eventually our digging arms gave out and the sand began collapsing into the deep and ever-enlarging hole, so we abandoned the skinny outer twigs of the lightning's course that dwindled down to next-to-nothing. I had a cigar box full of curiosities with which to barter for my badly needed rock-hound hammer. But this just didn't begin to compare to the thrill of discovery or the new-found respect and understanding of the elements. I don't think even my world-class grandfather could have pumped his lungs and stoked the furnace high enough to blast this glassy, solid connection between the realms.

Always before I had seen the sky as a two-dimensional backdrop – as if completely divorced from the earth and the ground beneath – a remote and distant entity requiring wings to touch or experience. Suddenly it was abundantly clear that there was a distinct and ferocious interaction between earth and sky, and I had hard fast, fulgurite evidence to prove it. Always before, with my nose pressed to the storm-sprayed screen, I had laughed at lightning as just an invigorating rush that did little more than blow out the street lamp across the way, or possibly somewhere torched a hapless tree.

* * *

Years later I had dropped out of art school and moved to the big cities. I illustrated for the big publishers and on my own time began painting with far too many smudgy yellowed brushstrokes to represent the day-glow mustard hues of smog. So to Maine we came for the gem-quality skies, which are often looted by the infamous weather, yet still worth the price. But it took me a full ten years of osmosis living here to even try and paint this artists' pot of gold. Suddenly my state-of-the-art colors couldn't hold up to the challenge of such a shimmering spectrum. The ocean was not a blue from any tube, but instead a magnifying mirror of a sky that went off the scale of the color wheel, and I had met my match.

On one of our sun-hungry winter trips, I discovered natural ochres and raw mineral pigments – good old fashioned earth colors long used by the Indians of the southwest. I was jumping for joy, but I had no (*most necessary*) blues for skies until a kind Hopi woman gave me some azurite chunks which I pulverized and turned into paint. But this only whetted my appetite for ever-finer mediums with which to express my admiration for nature's integrity. Finally and reluctantly I gave in and did some actual book-readin' research, and learned that the ancients had known the answers all along. They too had unearthed the sky, and through painstaking work, extracted the finest true blue from lapis lazuli, an exotic semi-precious stone once valued by artists more highly than gold. Science and synthetics still can't match the luminosity and sparkle of this, and other natural sources. Smirking, and tingling with a sense of *déja vu*, I suddenly knew that destiny had brought me full circle, like a paint-daubed pigeon, right back to my childhood passion for the real stuff, and I found yet again that Mother Nature had beat me there.

As for how they ever made the first straight line … I still can't draw one, and artist or not, nobody really can. Because whoever or whatever Creator, with infinite wisdom and intuition, structured our entire physical universe on the idea of the circle – spheres, spirals, waves, orbits, revolutions, cycles always and forever re-cycling whatever goes around to come around again. And we can see this so very clearly in the sinuous meanders of jet streams, the paisley-swirled storms, corkscrew hurricanes, the birth and rebirth of clouds and ever-returning raindrops all yielding to the call of the curve.

Sailing ships still won't fall off the flat, straight-lined edge of the earth, nor will we ever be banned from the sky. For the Earth and the Sky are truly wed, as inseparable spouses, each faithfully and spontaneously giving one to the other in an intimate dance of Life. That we should ever parcel out and sell fenced-off acres of sky would crush the spirit and break the trespassing hearts of all artists, for our earth-bound vision and palette of colors is determined by the rules of open sky. Our very inspiration is guided by the glow from above and the liberty to create within unconfined space. There is no more quixotic quest than to form such a perfect union of harmonious elements on our canvases of dreams.

★ ★ ★

Now that jet-finned 1950 is long past, and the digital warp of 2000 is at hand, I'm glad to have unearthed some primal bits of sky. For my fascination with the intricate details and exquisite patterns of nature is increasingly met with an utter reverence for the astounding miracle of it all. I don't think a million awe-struck artists such as I could ever paint a picture as spectacular as a galaxy-wide sky embracing, so fittingly, our planet. And yet, never giving up, we still try to pay homage and do justice to "The Web of Life." Our world of earth and sky is indeed an interactive, interdependent and perfectly functioning organism of vital systems which do not and cannot survive, one without the other.

I wonder if at the heart of this diverse "web" might be the very *essence of wildness* – that sacred and original secret formula of balanced perfection that we seem to yearn for, and eternally seek to emulate with art, and with science, hope to understand?

And could we ever behold a *wilder* or more engaging romance than that steamy ongoing affair between the modest Earth and the infatuated Sky?

Paul M. Breeden and his fellow artist wife Ann live in Sullivan, on the coast of Maine. Paul's natural history illustrations have been published for over thirty years in National Geographic, Audubon, Smithsonian, *etc., and throughout Europe. He, Ann, and his son Robert show their paintings and sculpture at their family gallery at Spring Woods. Among his other works, Paul has also written a yet-to-be-illustrated children's book about the sky. Of all the major projects of his career, he feels doing justice to* Soul of the Sky *to be the most challenging privilege yet.*

Paul included a note with the drawing that introduces this piece: "The big swirls are found in Acoma Pueblo Indian pottery designs from 'Sky City' in New Mexico. The lightning bolts are inspired by the works of Casas Grandes potters of Mata Ortiz, Mexico. The swirls and the stairstep designs depict clouds, and the vertical lines depict rain."

David Clark

TWENTY FOUR EVENINGS AGO I went for a walk down the dirt road in front of my house. I passed by a large open shelter where two farmers store the tractor, the combine, and the other essentials of tending several hundred acres of soybeans, cotton, and peanuts which lay on either side of the dirt road. These open fields have been farmland since strong men and oxen cleared out the virgin pine forest in the 1850s. From that point forward these fields have raised generation after generation of cotton, peanuts, and the families who tended them.

It just so happened that there were two trucks pulled up to the shelter. The two farmers were leaning on the hood of one of the trucks.

I made a turn into the field. The two men watched me under the brims of their hats – this long-haired fellow walking towards them with his dog.

When I got close enough to trip some sort of invisible signal, both of the men simultaneously pushed their hats back and stood up straight. They looked me dead in the eye, nodded, and said, "Howdy."

After introductions, I commented that it looked like we had gotten some rain.

"Yep, we got right at two inches. It sure was pretty."

"It sure was. It couldn't have come at a better time. If we can just get another rain like that in the next ten to fourteen days I'll make the best crop I've ever had."

We were standing next to a large diesel irrigation pump. "It'd be nice to not have to use this thing any more this year. I'm glad I got it, but it just ain't the same."

Fifteen days later a friend and I were walking on the same dirt road. It was now dry as a bone and dusty since those "ten to fourteen days" had passed with cloudless skies.

The grave truth that our sandy South Georgia soil is at any given time one week away from a drought became a coating one wished to spit off one's tongue. The August sun had baked the Volkswagen-sized Amphibian Opry House below the culvert from the western field, changing it into a crusty hole in the ground.

The two days before, the diesel pump had started running and hadn't stopped since. A great stream of irrigation water was shooting out over a small section of this huge field in an effort to provide the water so essential to these crops which were all in their final stages of providing the livelihood for these men and their families.

As we walked out from the house that early evening, we saw one of the farmers in the field at the sprinkler head. He appeared to be just watching the water.

He came driving out of the field and stopped to speak to us.

"How's it going?"

"Well, I'm gettin' a little water out there. I'm just not sure it'll be enough." He had the same worried, drawn look that most of this rural community was wearing.

A car pulled up beside us and stopped. "Where you been?" It was the farmer's wife.

"I been adjusting that sprinkler head."

"Well, you need to come home for supper. I was worried about you." She had the same look as the farmer.

Both of their vehicles were dusty. The man and his wife looked tired and anxious. Their lifetime of working the land wasn't very much fun right this minute.

The farmer smiled at us and said, "Welp, I guess I better get going."

We walked up the road and passed by the large diesel irrigation pump he was hoping not to use. It was roaring full steam.

My friend asked, "What's that noise?"

"That's the sound of a farmer trying to feed his fourteen-year-old daughter and ten-year-old son; of a farmer trying to hold on to this land which has been in his family for a hundred years. That's the sound of a farmer down on his knees asking God for rain."

Every evening since, I've seen the farmer, standing near the large sprinkler head as it makes its journey around the field. I've noticed that the field seems bigger to me as I compare it to the size of the area covered by the water.

This is the twenty-fourth morning since the farmer told me of his hopes of getting two inches of rain within "ten to fourteen days." For the first time in twenty-four mornings, it's cloudy. The September air has that clammy feeling I can remember from grammar school, when it would rain and we'd have to stay inside at recess.

And the whole county is standing on the porch, peering out the windows, going to switch off the irrigation pump, silently cheering on God as if he were a ball carrier bringing that two inches of rain to the goal line of their cotton field.

In this rural county where virtually everyone is either a farmer or kin to one, everyone is standing together looking at the sky, waiting for the rain as if it were a parade that was still just a few blocks away.

David Clark lives in Cochran, Georgia. His work appears in Southern Living, Charleston Magazine, Cigar Lifestyles, Peanut Farmer Magazine, *and numerous newspapers. He can be heard from time to time on* Peach State Public Radio, The Weather Notebook, *and* All Things Considered.

HOW TO WATCH THE SKY

Diane Ackerman

I AM SITTING AT THE EDGE of the continent, at Point Reyes National Seashore, the peninsula north of San Francisco, where the land gives way to the thrall of the Pacific and the arching blue conundrum of the sky. When cricket-whine, loud as a buzz saw, abruptly quits, only bird calls map the quiet codes of daylight. A hawk leans into nothingness, peeling a layer of flight from thin air. At first it flaps hard to gain a little altitude, then finds a warm updraft and cups the air with its wings, spiraling up in tight circles as it eyes the ground below for rodents or rabbits. Banking a little wider, it turns slowly, a twirling parasol. The hawk knows instinctively that it will not fall. The sky is the one visual constant in all our lives, a complex backdrop to our every venture, thought, and emotion. Yet we tend to think of it as invisible – an absence, not a substance. Though we move through air's glassy fathoms, we rarely picture it as the thick heavy arena it is. We rarely wonder about the blue phantasm we call the sky. *"Skeu,"* I say out loud, the word that our ancient ancestors used; I try to utter it as they might have, with fear and wonder: *"Skeu."* Actually, it was their word for a covering of any sort. To them, the sky was a roof of changing colors. Small wonder they billeted their gods there, like so many quarrelsome neighbors who, in fits of temper, hurled lightning bolts instead of crockery.

Look at your feet. You are standing in the sky. When we think of the sky, we tend to look up, but the sky actually begins at the earth. We walk through it, yell into it, rake leaves, wash the dog, and drive cars in it. We breathe it deep within us. With every breath, we inhale millions of molecules of sky, heat them briefly, and then exhale them back into the world. At this moment, you are breathing some of the same molecules once breathed by Leonardo da Vinci, William Shakespeare, Anne Bradstreet, or Colette. Inhale deeply. Think of *The Tempest*. Air works the bellows of our lungs, and it powers our cells. We say "light as air," but there is nothing lightweight about our atmosphere, which weighs 5,000 trillion tons. Only a clench as stubborn as gravity's could hold it to the earth; otherwise it would simply float away and seep into the cornerless expanse of space.

Without thinking, we often speak of "an empty sky." But the sky is never empty. In a mere ounce of air, there are 1,000 billion trillion gyrating atoms made up of oxygen, nitrogen, and hydrogen, each a menagerie of electrons, quarks, and ghostly neutrinos. Sometimes we marvel at how "calm" the day is, or how "still" the night. Yet there is no stillness in the sky, or anywhere else where life and matter meet. The air is always vibrant and aglow, full of volatile gases, staggering spores, dust, viruses, fungi, and animals, all stirred by a skirling and relentless wind. There are active flyers like butterflies, birds, bats, and insects, who ply the air roads; and there are passive flyers like autumn leaves, pollen, or milkweed pods, which just float. Beginning at the earth and stretching up in all directions, the sky is the thick, twitching realm in which we live. When we say that our distant ancestors crawled out onto the land, we forget to add that they really moved from one ocean to another, from the upper fathoms of water to the deepest fathoms of air.

The prevailing winds here are from the west, as I can see from the weird and wonderful shapes of the vegetation along the beach. A light steady breeze blowing off the Pacific has swept back the wild grasses into a sort of pompadour. A little farther back, in a more protected glade, I find a small clump of them, around which a circle runs in the dirt. It looks as if someone pressed a cookie cutter down in the ground, but the wind alone has done it, blowing the grass around and turning it into a natural protractor. We think of the wind as a destructive force – a sudden funnel that pops a roof off a schoolhouse in Oklahoma – but the wind is also a gradual and powerful mason that carves cliffs, erodes hillsides, re-creates beaches, moves trees and rocks down mountains or across rivers. Wind creates waves, as in the sensuously rippling dunes of Death Valley or along the changing shorelines. The wind hauls away the topsoil as if it were nothing more than a dingy tablecloth on the checkerboard fields of the Midwest, creating a "dust bowl." It can power generators, gliders, windmills, kites, sailboats. It sows seeds and pollen. It sculpts the landscape. Along rugged coasts, one often sees trees dramatically carved by the relentless wind.

The north wind is shown on ancient maps as a plump-cheeked man with tousled hair and a strained expression, blowing as hard as he can. According to Homer, the god Aeolus lived in a palatial cave, where he kept the winds tied up in a leather bag. He gave the bag to Odysseus to power his ship, but when Odysseus's comrades opened the bag the winds raced free throughout the world, squabbling and whirling and generally wreaking havoc. "The children of morning," Hesiod called the Greek winds. To the ancient Chinese, *fung* meant both wind and breath, and there were many words for the wind's temperaments. *Tiu* meant "to move with the wind like a tree." *Yao* was the word for when something floated on the breeze like down. The names of winds are magical, and tell a lot about the many moods the sky can take. There's Portugal's hillside *vento coado*; Japan's demonic *tsumuji*, or soft pine-grove-loving *matsukaze*; Australia's balmy *brickfielder* (which first described dust storms blowing off brickyards near Sydney); America's moist warm *chinook* drifting in from the sea, and named after the language of Indians who settled Oregon; or snow-clotted *blizzard*, or fierce *Santa Ana*, or Hawaii's humid *waimea*; North Africa's hot, sand-laden desert *simoom* (from the Aramaic word *samma*, "poison"); Argentina's baking, depleting *zonda*, which pours down from the Andes to sweep the pampas; the Nile's dark, gloomy *haboob*; Russia's gale-force *buran*, bringing a storm in the summer or a blizzard in the winter; Greece's refreshing summer *etesian*; Switzerland's warm, gusty *foehn* blowing off the leeward slopes of a mountain; France's dry cold *mistral* ("master wind") squalling through the Rhône Valley and down to the Mediterranean coast; India's notorious *monsoon*, whose very name means a whole season of monsoons; the Cape of Good Hope's *bull's-eye squall*; Alaska's petulant *williwaw*; Gibraltar's easterly-blowing *datoo*; Spain's mellifluous *solano*; the Caribbean's *hurricane* (derived from the Taino word *huracan*, which means "evil spirit"); Sweden's gale-level *frisk vind*; China's whispering *I tien tien fung*, or first autumn breeze, the *sz*.

Storms have been fretting the coast here for days, and now thick gray clouds stagger across this sky. I watch mashed-potato heaps of *cumulus* (a word that means "pile") and broad bands of *stratus* (which means "stretched out"). As author James Trefil once observed, a cloud is a sort of floating lake. When rising warm air collides with descending cold air, the water falls, as it does now. I take shelter on a porch, while a real toad-strangler starts, a full-blooded, hell-for-leather thunderstorm, during which the sky crackles and throbs. Lightning appears to plunge out of it, a pitchfork stabbing into the ground. In fact, it sends down a short electrical scout first, and the earth replies by arcing a long bolt up toward the sky, heating the air so fast that it explodes into a shock wave, or *thunder*, as we call it. Counting the seconds between a lightning flash and the thunder, I then divide by five, and get a rough idea of how far away it is – seven miles. In one second, sound travels 1,100 feet. If the lightning flash and the thunder arrive at the same time, one doesn't have much of a chance to count. In a little while the storm quiets, as the thunder bumpers roll farther up the coast. But some clouds still stalk the sky. A cloud rhinoceros metamorphoses into a profile of Eleanor Roosevelt; then a bowl of pumpkins; then a tongue-wagging dragon. Parading hugely across the sky, clouds like these have squatted above people of all times and countries. How many vacant afternoons people have passed watching the clouds drift by. The ancient Chinese amused themselves by finding shapes in the clouds just as Inuits, Bantus, and Pittsburghers do now. Sailors, generals, farmers, ranchers, and others have always consulted the crystal ball of the sky to foretell the weather (lens-shaped clouds – severe winds aloft; dappled or "mackerel" sky – rain is near; low, thick, dark, blanketlike clouds – a stormy cold front may be coming), devising jingles, maxims, and elaborate cloud charts and atlases, graphics as beautiful as they are useful. On a train through Siberia, Laurens van der Post looked out the window at the huge expanse of flat country and endless sky. "I thought I had never been to any place with so much sky and space around it," he writes in *Journey into Russia*, and was especially startled by "the immense thunder clouds moving out of the dark towards the sleeping city resembling, in the spasmodic lightning, fabulous swans beating towards us on hissing wings of fire." As van der Post watched the lightning from the train, the Russian friend accompanying him explained that they had a special word in his language for just that scene: *Zarnitsa*.

Throughout time and place, people have been obsessed with the many moods of the sky. Not just because their crops and journeys depended on the weather, but because the sky is such a powerful symbol. The sky that gods inhabit, the sky whose permanence we depend on and take for granted, as if it really were a solid, vaulted ceiling on which stars were painted, as our ancestors thought. The sky that can fall in nursery rhymes. In the nuclear disarmament marches of the sixties, some people wore signs that read: CHICKEN LITTLE WAS RIGHT. We picture the sky as the final resting place of those we love, as if their souls were perfumed aerosol. We bury them among pine needles and worms, but in our imaginations we give them a lighter-than-air journey into some recess of the sky from which they will watch over us. "High" is where lofty sentiments dwell, where the "high and mighty" live, where choirs of angels sing. I don't know why the sky symbolizes our finest ideals and motives, unless, lacking in self-confidence, we think our acts of mercy, generosity, and heroism are not intrinsic qualities, not characteristics human beings alone can muster, but temporary gifts from some otherworldly power situated in the sky. Stymied by events, or appalled by human nature, we sometimes roll our eyes upward, to where we believe our fate is dished out in the mansions of the stars.

Driving four hours south, along spectacular cliffs and a wild and dramatic ocean where sea otters bob in the kelp beds, sea lions bark, harbor seals clump together like small mountain ranges, and pelagic cormorants, sanderlings, murres, and other seabirds busily nest, I pause on a wind-ripped slope of Big Sur. A Monterey pine leans out over the Pacific, making a ledge for the sunset. The pummeling gales have strangled its twigs and branches on the upwind side, and it looks like a shaggy black finger pointing out to sea. People pull up in cars, get out, stand and stare. Nothing need be said. We all understand the visual nourishment we share. We nod to one another. The cottony blue sky and dark-blue sea meet at a line sharp as a razor's edge. Why is it so thrilling to see a tree hold pieces of sky in its branches, and hear waves crash against a rocky shore, blowing spray high into the air, as the seagulls creak? Of the many ways to watch the sky, one of the most familiar is through the filigree limbs of a tree, or around and above trees; this has much to do with how we actually see and observe the sky. Trees conduct the eye from the ground up to the heavens, link the detailed temporariness of life with the bulging blue abstraction overhead. In Norse legend, the huge ash tree Yggdrasil, with its great arching limbs and three swarming roots, stretched high into the sky, holding the universe together, connecting earth to both heaven and hell. Mythical animals and demons dwelt in the tree; at one of its roots lay the well of Mimir, the source of all wisdom, from which the god Odin drank in order to become wise, even though it cost him the loss of an eye. We find trees offering us knowledge in many of the ancient stories and legends, perhaps because they alone seem to unite the earth and the sky – the known, invadable world with everything that is beyond our grasp and our power.

Today the ocean pours darkly, with a white surf pounding over and over. Close to the shore, the thick white wave-spume looks applied by a palette knife. The damp, salty wind rustles like taffeta petticoats. One gull finds a shellfish and begins picking it apart, while the others fly after it and try to snatch the food away, all of them squeaking like badly oiled machinery.

When I was in Istanbul many years ago, I marveled at the way the onion-shaped mosques carved the sky between them. Instead of seeing a skyline, as one would in New York or San Francisco, one saw only the negative space between the swirling, swooping, spiraling minarets and bulbous domes. But here one sees the silhouette of distinctive trees against the sky: Scotch pine, which has a long stem with a roundish top resembling a child's rattle; tall, even, rice-grain-shaped cypress and spruce. Farther north stand the sequoias, the heaviest living things to inhabit the planet. The talcy-leaved eucalyptus, nonnative trees that are so hardy and fast-growing they've taken over whole forests in California, look like bedraggled heads of freshly shampooed hair. In the fall and winter, one can find among their branches long garlands of monarch butterflies, hanging on by their feet, which have prongs like grappling hooks. Each year, a hundred million migrate as much as four thousand miles from the northern United States and Canada to overwinter on the

California coast. They cluster to keep warm. Butterflies seem to prefer the oily mentholated groves, the fumes of which keep away most insects and birds. Blue jays occasionally attack the monarchs when they leave their garland to sip nectar or sit out in the open and spread their wings wide as solar collectors. Monarch larvae eat the leaves of milkweed, a poisonous, digitalislike plant, to which they are immune, but which makes *them* poisonous; and birds quickly learn that eating monarchs will make them sick. If you see a monarch flying around with a wedge-shaped piece of wing missing, you are most likely looking at a veteran of an uninformed bird's attack. When I was helping to tag monarchs, I saw just such a female trembling on the porch floor outside my motel-room window. A huge blue jay in a nasty temper perched on the porch rail, screeching and flapping, and getting ready to dive at the monarch again. Though I usually know better than to intrude in nature's doings, my instincts took over and I rushed outside, lunged at the blue jay to punch it in the chest, just as it leapt up with a great squawk and flap, truly terrified by my sudden attack. The butterfly stood her ground and shook, and I picked her up carefully, checked to see if she were pregnant by pressing her abdomen gently between my thumb and forefinger, feeling for a hard pellet. She wasn't, and the missing wedge of wing didn't look too bad, so I carried her to the base of a tree, at the top of which swayed a long orange string of monarchs. Then I held her above my open mouth and breathed warm air over her body, to help heat her flying muscles since it was a chilly morning, and tossed her into the air. She fluttered right up to her cluster, and, as I walked back to my room, I saluted her. The blue jay was still shrieking bloody murder, and then I saw it fly out of the yard with strong, confident beats.

At Big Sur, the hawks are working the thermals like barnstormers, swooping and banking as they ride invisible towers of warm, rising air above the sun-heated ground. Birds are so nimble and adroit. Each species has its own architecture, flight habits, and talents to make the most of the sky, which they sometimes reveal in their silhouettes. On some owls, for instance, the leading edge of the primary feathers is softly fringed to muffle the sound of their approach. Finches flap hard a few beats, then close their wings and rest a little. Turtledoves flap continuously when they're flying. Peregrine falcons fold in their wings when they dive. Swifts, which average about twenty-five mph, have very pointy wings that make them sleeker by cutting down on drag as they dart and glide. At the Grand Canyon, you can see them working the canyon walls like small aerobats.

Our sky is also filled with "passive flyers." Female ash trees loose their winged "keys," and aspens and others produce long catkins that drop and blizzard across the ground. Maples launch tadpole-shaped seeds that fall whirligig down, all blade, all propeller, like small autogyros. Thanks to the wind, the sex lives of many plants have changed. Dandelions, milkweed, thistles, cottonwoods, and others have evolved wind-riders in the shape of parachutes or sails. Pine, spruce, hemlock, maple, oak, and ragweed don't have flamboyant flowers, but they don't need them to divert a bird or bee. The wind is go-between enough. Plants can't court, or run away from a threat, so they've devised ingenious ways to exploit their environment and animals. Pollen grains may be as small as one ten-thousandth of an inch in diameter, yet they must travel uncertain winds and strike home. Using a wind tunnel, Karl Niklas, a Cornell scientist, recently discovered that plants aren't just hobos, hoping their pollen will catch a passing breeze and get off at the right stop. Niklas found that the pine cone has evolved an architecture perfect for capturing wind from any direction: a turbine shape, with petal-blades that spin the air all around it. Like a planet, the pine cone wraps itself in an atmosphere of rapidly moving air, with, just below the upper, swirling layer, a still and vacant layer. When pollen falls from the rapid layer to the still layer, it cascades right down into the cone. Niklas also tested the airflow dynamics of the jojoba plant, which uses two rabbit-ear-shaped leaves to direct air, with results that show similar finesse.

In allergy season, pollen makes me (and millions of others) sneeze a little, and my eyes sometimes itch so that I can't wear my contact lenses. But I like knowing that all this mischief happens just because of shape. Tiny Sputniks traveling through the lower sky, some pollen looks like balls covered with spikes. Others are as football-shaped as the pupils of alligators. Pine pollen is round, with what looks like a pair of ears attached to each side. Their shapes make them move or fly at different speeds and in different patterns, and there's little danger of the wrong pollen swamping the wrong plant. It's odd to think of the sky having niches, but it does; even the wind has niches.

As night falls on Big Sur, all the soot of the world seems to pour down into the sunset. A swollen yellow doubloon drops slowly into the ocean, shimmer by shimmer, as if swallowed whole. Then, at the horizon, a tiny green ingot hovers for a second, and vanishes. The "green flash" people call it, with mystical solemnity. But it is the briefest flash of green, and this is the first time in all my sunset-watching that I've seen it. Green, azure, purple, red: How lucky we are to live on a planet with colored skies. Why is the sky blue? The sun's white light is really a bouquet of colored rays, which we classify into a spectrum of six colors. When white light collides with atoms of gases that make up the atmosphere – primarily oxygen and nitrogen – as well as with dust particles and moisture in the air, blue light, the most energetic light of the visible spectrum, is scattered. The sky seems to be full of blue. This is particularly true when the sun is overhead, because the light rays have a shorter distance to travel. The red rays are longer, and penetrate the atmosphere better. By the time the sun sets, one side of the Earth is turning away from the sun; the light has to travel farther, at an angle, through even more dust, water vapor, and air molecules; the blue rays scatter even more and the red rays remain, still traveling. The sun may appear magnified into a swollen ghost, or slightly elliptical, or even above the horizon when it's really below it, thanks to refraction, the bending of light waves. What we see is a glorious red sunset, especially if prowling clouds reflect the changing colors. The last color that plows through the atmosphere without being scattered is green, so sometimes we see a green flash right after the sun disappears. In space, the air appears to be black because there is no dust to scatter the blue light.

At Big Sur lighthouse, perched on a distant promontory, a beacon flashes to warn ships away from the coast and sandbanks, its light zooming out to them at 186,000 miles per second. The searchlight of the sun takes about eight minutes to reach Earth. And the light we see from the North Star set sail in the days of Shakespeare. Just think how straight the path of light is. Pass sunlight through a prism, though, and the light bends. Because each ray bends a different amount, the colors separate into a band. Many things catch the light prismatically – fish scales, the mother-of-pearl inside a limpet shell, oil on a slippery road, a dragonfly's wings, opals, soap bubbles, peacock feathers, the grooves in gramophone records, metal that's lightly tarnished, the neck of a hummingbird, the wing cases of beetles, spiders' webs smeared with dew – but perhaps the best known is water vapor. When it's raining but the sun is shining, or at a misty waterfall, sunlight hits the prismlike drops of water and is split into what we call a "rainbow." On such a day, rainbows are always about, hidden somewhere behind the skirts of the rain; but to see one best, you have to be positioned just right, with the sun behind you and low in the sky.

★   ★   ★

It is nighttime on the planet Earth. But that is only a whim of nature, a result of our planet rolling in space at 1,000 miles per minute. What we call "night" is the time we spend facing the secret reaches of space, where other solar systems and, perhaps, other planetarians dwell. Don't think of night as the absence of day; think of it as a kind of freedom. Turned away from our sun, we see the dawning of far-flung galaxies. We are no longer sun-blind to the star-coated universe we inhabit. The endless black, which seems to stretch forever between the stars and even backwards in time to the Big Bang, we call "infinity," from the French in-fini meaning unfinished or incomplete. Night is a shadow world. The only shadows we see at night are cast by the moonlight, or by artificial light, but night itself is a shadow.

In the country, you can see more stars, and the night looks like an upside-down well that deepens forever. If you're patient and wait until your eyes adjust to the darkness, you can see the Milky Way as a creamy smudge across the sky. Just as different cultures have connected the stars into different constellations, they've seen their own private dramas in the Milky Way. The "backbone of night" the Bushmen of the Kalahari call it. To the Swedes, it is the "winter street" leading to heaven. To the Hebridean islanders, the "pathway of the secret people." To the Norse, the "path of ghosts." To the Patagonians, obsessed with their flightless birds, "the White pampas where ghosts hunt rheas." But in the city you can see the major constellations more easily because there are fewer stars visible to distract you.

Wherever you are, the best way to watch stars is lying on your back. Tonight the half-moon has a Mayan profile. It looks luminous and shimmery, a true beacon in the night, and yet I know its brilliance is all borrowed light. By day, if I held a mirror and bounced a spot of sunlight around the trees, I would be mimicking how the moon reflects light, having none of its own to give. Above me, between Sagittarius and Aquarius, the constellation Capricorn ambles across the sky. The Aztecs pictured it as a whale (*cipactli*), the East Indians saw an antelope (*makaram*), the Greeks labeled it "the gate of the gods," and to the Assyrians it was a goat-fish (*munaxa*). Perhaps the best-known star in the world is the North Star, or Polaris, though of course it has many other names; to the Navaho, it is "The Star That Does Not Move," to the Chinese, the "Great Imperial Ruler of Heaven."

Throughout time, people have looked up at the sky to figure out where they were. When I was a girl, I used to take an empty can, stretch a piece of tinfoil over one end and pierce pinholes in it in the outline of a constellation; then I'd shine a flashlight in the other end, and have my own private planetarium. How many wanderers, lost on land or sea, have waited till night to try and chart their way home with help from the North Star. Locating it as they did connects us across time to those early nomads. First you find the Big Dipper and extend a line through the outer two stars of its ladle. Then you'll see that the North Star looks like a dollop of cream fallen from the upside-down Dipper. If the Big Dipper isn't visible, you can find the North Star by looking for Cassiopeia, a constellation just below Polaris that's shaped like a W or an M, depending on the time you see it. To me, it usually looks like a butterfly. Because the Earth revolves, the stars seem to drift from east to west across the sky, so another way to tell direction is to keep your eye on one bright star in particular; if it appears to rise, then you're facing east. If it seems to be falling, you're facing west. When I was a Girl Scout, we found our direction during the day by putting a straight stick in the ground. Then we'd go about our business for a few hours and return when the stick cast a shadow about six inches long. The sun would have moved west, and the shadow would be pointing east. Sometimes we used a wristwatch as a compass: Place the watch face up, with the hour hand pointing toward the sun. Pick up a pine needle or twig and hold it upright at the edge of the dial so that it casts a shadow along the hour hand. South will be halfway between the hour hand and twelve o'clock. There are many other ways to tell direction, of course, since roaming is one of the things human beings love to do best – but only if they can count on getting home safely. If you see a tree standing out in the open, with heavy moss on one side, that side is probably north, since moss grows heaviest on the shadiest side of a tree. If you see a tree stump, its rings will probably be thicker on the sunny side, or south. You can also look up at the tops of pine trees, which mainly point east. Or, if you happen to know where the prevailing wind is coming from, you can read direction from the wind-bent grasses.

It's November. The Leonids are due in Leo. Pieces of comet that fall mainly after sunset or before sunrise, they appear in the same constellations each year at the same time. In Antarctica, I had hoped to see *auroras*, veils of light caused by the solar wind bumping into the earth's magnetic field and leaving a gorgeous shimmer behind. But our days were mainly sun-perfect, and our nights a grisly gray twilight. In the evening, the sea looked like pounded gunmetal, but there were no auroras to make glitter paths overhead. Here is how Captain Robert Scott described one display in June 1911:

> *The eastern sky was massed with swaying auroral light ... fold on fold the arches and curtains of vibrating luminosity rose and spread across the sky, to slowly fade and yet again spring to glowing life.*
>
> *The brighter light seemed to flow, now to mass itself in wreathing folds in one quarter, from which lustrous streamers shot upward, and anon to run in waves through the system of some dimmer figure....*
>
> *It is impossible to witness such a beautiful phenomenon without a sense of awe, and yet this sentiment is not inspired by its brilliancy but rather by its delicacy in light and colour, its transparency, and above all by its tremulous evanescence of form.*

Tonight Mars glows like a steady red ember. Though only a dot of light in the sky, it is in my mind a place of blustery plains, volcanoes, rift valleys, sand dunes, wind-carved arches, dry river beds, and brilliant white polar caps that wax and wane with the seasons. There may even have been a climate there once, and running water. Soon Venus will appear as a bright silvery light, as it usually does about three hours after sunset or before sunrise. With its gauzy white face, it looks mummified in photos, but I know that impression is given by cloud banks full of acids floating above a surface where tricks of light abound and the temperatures are hot enough to melt lead. There are many kinds of vision – literal, imaginative, hallucinatory; visions of greatness or of great possibilities. Although I can't see the steady light of other planets just yet, I know they are there all the same, along with the asteroids, comets, distant galaxies, neutron stars, black holes, and other phantoms of deep space. And I picture them with a surety Walt Whitman understood when he proclaimed: "The bright suns I see and the dark suns I cannot see are in their place."

Sunrise. Darkness begins to wash out of the sky. A thick lager of fog sits in the valley like the chrysalis of a moth. Venus, Mercury, and Saturn burn bright silver holes in the slowly bluing sky. The stars have vanished, because by the time starlight gets to Earth it's too dim to be seen during the daylight. Two black shapes in the fog reel into focus as cows. A calf reveals itself. Learning about the world is like this – watching and waiting for shapes to reveal themselves in the fog of our experience. A wan sky curdles with gauzy streaks of cloud. The land is veiled in mist. The highest hill looks like a train's smokestack: Clouds trail behind it. Now the cloud world that was horizontal becomes vertical as cumulus begin to rise over the mountain. Venus throbs, a broken lighthouse in the western sky. A nation of cloud tepees rises along the top of the ridge. The first hawk of the day glides on cool air, wings arched. The dew sits in round, bluish drops on the clover-rich grass. A squadron of eighteen pelicans flies in a long check mark overhead, turns on edge and vanishes, turns again and tilts back into sight. A huge pillow of fog rolls through the valley. The cows disappear, but the sky grows bluer; Venus fades, white clouds begin to form, the fog lifts like a fever, a house and more cows appear. A lone, lightning-struck tree stands like a totem pole on a hillside, the light quickens, and birds begin their earnest songs, as the first yellow floats up like egg yolk over the ledge of the world, and then the sun is a canary singing light.

From A Natural History of the Senses. *Used by permission of the Author.*

Diane Ackerman was born in Waukegan, Illinois. She received her M.A., M.F.A. and Ph.D. from Cornell University. Her works of nonfiction include A Natural History of the Senses, A Natural History of Love; *and* The Curious Naturalist. *Her poetry has been published in many leading literary journals.*

Ms. Ackerman has received the Academy of American Poets' Peter I. B. Lavan Award, and grants from the National Endowment for the Arts and the Rockefeller Foundation among other prizes and awards, and she has taught at a variety of universities, including Columbia and Cornell. She writes regularly for The New York Times, Parade, The New Yorker, *and* National Geographic *and other journals, where her essays about nature and human nature have been the subject of much praise.*

Craig Werth

I WAS STANDING beside our family van draining the melted ice from our cooler when a somber looking young couple belonging to the car next to us returned from their hike along the fogged-in New Brunswick coast. The man looked at the yellow sea kayaks cradled on our roof with friendly envy and asked if we'd gone kayaking. I suppose this wasn't such a silly question given the weather of the moment. "We've been out a few times," I said.

"We just arrived today. Has it been foggy here all week?"

"We arrived yesterday morning and it was sunny and clear."

"It was sunny yesterday? Well I guess we brought the fog with us then."

"So you're the ones who did it," I joked back, "thanks a heaping lot." He smiled weakly but looked genuinely guilty, and clearly disappointed as he unlocked the car doors and the two sank into their seats. The gray, moisture laden air had put both a figurative and literal damper on this couple's holiday. Not long ago I might have shared their reaction to this atmospheric imposition – before I developed my appreciation for the gentle blanketing ... the close focus ... and the volumes of rich, intrinsic scenery offered up to us in fog.

Some five years earlier, I'd embarked on one of my very first sea kayaking outings in the Deer Isle archipelago in the Gulf of Maine. It was the summer of my twentieth high school reunion. I'd just returned from the nostalgic trip down to the Catskill Mountains in New York having gone to the reunion solo, leaving my wife and son behind in New Hampshire. I had wanted to wrestle with the churning of mid-life alone, even though I knew it would be a risky ride on the time machine back to an era of blissful naiveté and magical, heart-wrenching first love. Back from the reunion only a couple of days, all stirred up with life choice questions, ghosts of lost dreams, and a host of existential naggings, I joined three male friends for a long-scheduled paddle in this heaven of seascape. My goal was to lose my unsettled self in the beauty and effort of paddling in these waters.

The Deer Isle area must be among the most magnificent zones on the planet. The sea there is scattered with islands – hundreds of them – of all shapes and sizes. Some are large and populated, some are heavily forested, supporting wild deer and sheep populations, others are minor humps composed of bare, coarse rocks devoid of obvious life but for wisps of eternally optimistic grasses giving it their best shot at survival.

Relatively new to this mode of sport and transportation, I'd read up on sea kayaking a bit. I got a book on land and sea navigation, bought a compass for the kayak deck, studied charts of the area. I'd done my part, at least that which was in my control, and I wished for one thing above all else in return: fair weather. Like rain on the proverbial parade, I did not want fog out on the water. Not only would its intrusive hand hide this postcard-worthy scenery, but it would sorely test my tenderfoot status as an aspiring navigator of the sea.

My wish was granted upon arrival in Stonington, our paddle departure point. The late afternoon was crisp and clear. A warm and gentle breeze brushed the water's surface just enough to give it a soft, uniformly fluffy look. If sea water could come fresh out of the clothes dryer, it would look like this. We loaded the boats and walked them slowly to the water's edge, stretching shoulder, arm, and hand muscles with the weight of craft and cargo, put on our various kayaking-guy hats, and propelled our boats forth with the strong and steady paddle strokes of a fresh, green crew.

Our first destination was a relatively large island less than a mile from shore, a clearly visible, big, fat target. Even so, I checked my compass bearing to practice my spotty navigation knowledge (I'd paid $65 for the thing and needed to pretend it was useful from the start). With a more than fair chance at accuracy – something like throwing a dart at a billboard – I keenly observed that, sure enough, the land mass straight ahead of us was just about exactly where it was supposed to be. Yep, we ought to hold this bearing of 112 degrees. Either that or head for that enormous clump of rocks and trees straight ahead of us. Yessir … and then if we were to make a return trip from the island it would be … let's see … 112 plus 180 or … exactly 292 degrees to get back to the starting point. Or we could just head for our blue van, its windshield now shining like a beacon from the shore.

I knew that Maine's coast is famous for changing weather. For waves that rise up with no warning. For fog that rolls in on a whim, fog thick enough to scoop up and put into a zip-lock bag as a souvenir. I knew this, but like a spoiled child, I felt entitled to perfect weather. I expected God and whoever else serves on the committee to bear this in mind when planning the weather for my paddling days.

There was a time when I actually sought out fog … of a kind. During my childhood on Long Island, a few times every sticky summer, without warning, you'd hear the cry ring through our tight-packed suburban neighborhood: *"Fog Man!"* I'd grab the handlebars of my red bomber of a bike and leap onto the saddle, pedaling before my butt hit the seat. Within two blocks about a dozen other fog soldiers hit the pedals as well. We'd crank over lawn and curb between parked Ramblers and Chevy station wagons to convene directly behind the slow-moving truck of the mosquito fogger guy and cruise in loose formation within the clouds of toxic mist. Apparently with different sensibilities in the early 60s, not a single parent discouraged this practice.

We must have inhaled quarts of insect killing brew for the delight of traveling in fog, our quiet, too-familiar neighborhood transformed for some magical minutes into a world of dangerous wonder and fascination. It seems that I escaped all but two lasting side effects – a nagging case of male-pattern baldness and the tendency to forget many things my wife would prefer I remember. I suppose this childhood attraction reveals a fascination with fog, but that was fog on *my* terms, fog I could banish with a slowing of the pedal – not the sort you find in Mother Nature.

We completed the crossing to our fish-in-a-barrel target island and set up camp, blessed with a first day of fine weather. Feeling satisfied and catered to, I settled into my sleeping bag to rest my paddling bones and recharge my navigation master mind. I drifted off with images of sun's dawning and a naive spirit of readiness for the journey forth.

Sometime during the night, I became aware of the change. I felt something cool and wet layering over me in my half-sleep – folding ribbons of thin moisture, vapor tendrils flowing into my nostrils, curling the sparse remainder of my hair, and dampening my scalp.

By sunrise, or what I could sense of it, visibility was down to something like 20 feet and dropping. After a light breakfast of margarine-laced cous-cous and hot chocolate, we gathered around a large, flat-topped stone to roll out a chart and plan our next move. Our original intention was to hopscotch a variety of islands doing little if any retracing, but we, certainly I, also dared to count on clear weather, against all good and common sense. No one made light of the low visibility on the water and I took some small comfort in the fact that we were all a bit anxious and wary.

Although not one of us had brought a fog horn to warn off kayak-crushing crafts, we each had a shrill, two-tone whistle that could help us find one another, giving us some chance of staying together, like a family of ducklings swimming in the same general direction. Because we were in an archipelago of islands, there was little chance of missing a targeted island and going straight out to sea. If we got lost we'd most likely bump into some other island, giving us a chance to puzzle over our location for a bit. More likely hazards included capsizing with no one near to help and little time to execute a solo escape from the hypothermic waters or collision with a motor boat that could come from any direction.

In what I'd heard to be the bible of sea kayaking, aptly titled *Sea Kayaking*, John Dowd calmly instructs the paddler in ways that fragile humans in soft-shelled vessels can adapt to the perils of the oceans. He illustrates his teachings with tales of encounters with everything from 15-foot walls of water to sharks. His treatment of fog caught my eye in particular. I wasn't ignoring the possibility of other dangers (I bet there isn't a sea kayaker who hasn't revisited the "dun dun dun dun" music from *Jaws*), but the solutions for dealing with those made more immediate sense. For walls of water, you take them head on, bracing with your paddle (and doing some combination of praying and kissing your kiester good bye – my addition). For sharks you wield your standard-issue shark stick (and, perhaps, keep a more tasty-looking paddling companion nearby – my addition).

But when dealing with a large approaching vessel that, due to heavy fog, you cannot see – and that cannot see you – Mr. Dowd's bible of sea kayaking recommends that you *paddle toward the sound*. Excuse me? And would Mr. Dowd advise hikers to charge directly toward the gnashing teeth of a roaring grizzly bear? "Naw, don't veer off, or back up, or even play dead – you march right on up there."

Well, Mr. Dowd has paddled all over the world for some 25 years and he's successfully negotiated each of these perils himself. Since my paddling experience was best measured in days and I'd practiced all my safety techniques in a warm, shallow pond, I returned to critically read some more. Turns out, Mr. Dowd can back up his advice with logic as well as experience. If you turn toward the sound you achieve two things: you make a much smaller target than with a broadside orientation and you give your eyes a chance to see whatever might appear from the fog. Paddling forward, even slowly, gives you the best turning capability to respond to an imminent collision. A stopped boat takes much more time and energy to get out of the way than one that has momentum. Well, I bought all this in theory, and hoped like heck I would never have to use it.

It was time to get the boats in the water. As we were rolling up the charts I realized that I wasn't clear about the plan we'd just agreed upon and I decided to speak up since my particular soft human body was on the line. We rolled the charts back out and I came up with the need for a lot of clarification. At first I didn't even agree with the majority opinion as to where we were on the island we were standing on, which can make an enormous difference when you choose a bearing toward somewhere else. Through further conversation, we all made contributions to a new collective perception and that "wait a minute" voice in me was satisfied, for now. In the ensuing silence I got my gear together and we moved our four boats to the water's edge.

Visibility was alternating between 10 and 30 feet as fog poured all around the island. I had a low-level anxiety quavering inside my body, consisting of some part fear and some part eager anticipation. After several more minutes of fiddling with equipment, probably as much from the standard fuss of people dealing with gear as from avoidance, we launched from the island and our challenge took a big leap from theory to practice.

The launch brings me to another personal historic reference to fog: a photographic enlargement of a black and white postcard presented to me in my youth, now hanging on the wall of my den. The caption reads "The Launching of 'The Fog Free Zone' – Exploit Harbor, New Foundland." In the center of this frozen moment, dwarfed by a huge white vessel, stands Skipper George Luff, my maternal great-grandfather, Granddad, as my mother remembers him, launching one of his hand-hewn sailing vessels into the momentarily calm but foreboding waters off the northern coast. I grew up with this remembrance mounted on my bedroom wall and I know it played a part in how I pieced together my thoughts of fear and fascination with the ocean, perhaps responding to a subliminal familial prejudice against the creature that is fog.

And now, some 70 years after my great-grandfather launched *The Fog Free Zone*, here I am launching my own little craft into the very weather Skipper George had named his great ship to ward off. (And I had to go and name my boat *Betty*.)

At first, we could not see each other – not consistently anyway. Ghosts of my partners would ebb and flow from view. Periodic voice check-ins quickly became necessary, at least until we adjusted to the inconsistent sightings, and silently organized ourselves so we each could stay aware of the paddler to the left and/or right of us by intermittent glimpses, the sounds of paddling, or the subtle sense of each others' presence. Our compass bearings all matched up well; it was crucial to check this as our readings could have varied enough to lead to annoying or even dangerous separation.

I thought of how rarely I've had to make my way forward in life without benefit of sight. I've played pin the tail on the donkey and swatted a piñata or two as a child. I've stumbled through the woods or my home at night (once I stepped through a wonderful classical guitar of mine after turning off the dresser light – I can still hear the sound of that beautiful instrument splintering around my foot). I suppose, in a way, I was still using my sight here, but the data it provided was scant. The color of fog was uniformly gray, offering no accurate sense of depth.

I soon realized that the fog was not only obstructing sight, but affecting sound as well. Auditory direction seemed unreliable and depth of sound was also difficult to discern. In this deepening sensual distortion and in the spaces between compass checks, glances for my friends, and surprisingly frequent time checks (the fog has a way of alternately stretching out and then truncating one's sense of time), my sight began its turn inward.

I've come to think of fog as a neutral thing. It's like a blank canvas – it becomes what we choose to shape and color it with: projected images, memories, imaginations, and even full-bodied emotional states. It can amplify and magnify these things, as if every suspended molecule of water is another mirror in a hall of a million mirrors, reflecting and revealing a fear, a hope, a dream, an insight, a vision. Letting loose a thought or feeling in such an environment can be unsettling, perhaps terrifying. Fog shares the reputation of the night. You sense that something's out there and the terrible truth is that the something is ... *me*. Maybe more of me than I'd care to discover or look at for very long.

But for me, on this particular day, the encounter with self was just what I needed. As I said up front, I'd come on this trip to escape from the churning of a 40-ish crisis. But here I was finding a magnified, concentrated version of the very thing I'd come here to lose. If I could trace the threads of all the thoughts and feelings I explored on this foggy crossing, I could write them in a book thicker than John Dowd's (though perhaps not so widely read). In the reflective space of the fog, the many blossoms of thought and feeling included these:

> ... *a careful accounting and review of my many fears and worries, which I was able to sort into the two dimensional billboard variety, and the real, 3-D ones worthy of concern and commitment of problem-solving energy ...*

> ... *a new perspective on my persistent mourning over the loss of my first love. I began to see my sense of loss of my high school sweetheart (freshly renewed at the reunion) for what it really was: sadness over the loss of the simpler, smaller, more magical time of my youth, when thoughts and feelings were sweet, close, and intense, and truths were easier to lean on ...*

> ... *images of my family – my wife and son – whom I too often took for granted, as if they were appendages to my life like an arm or a leg, appeared large and full and deep before me, the crystalline vision of them and their value in my life filling my eyes with tears.*

Like a water mammal surfacing, I'd occasionally leave the inner world of thought to see what was happening outside of me. The physical universe having narrowed to my boat and its contents, I'd notice something like my paddle stroke, and I became instantly aware of its inefficiency. With every stroke I'd been straining and grinding like a desperate man trying to get somewhere, anywhere, too fast. When I realized this, I experimented and quickly learned that a stroke with just about half the energy output yielded the same propulsion of the vessel forward. I found an optimal combination of finger, hand, arm, and back movement to get the most from each stroke with this particular paddle blade and this particular boat. What an enormous difference to save that energy, that life juice I'd been bleeding away. What a relief to feel more comfortable and efficient. How many other endeavors in my life were like this? How much did I strain and grind beyond what was necessary or beneficial? At the time, a few clear examples came to mind, and though the revelation has lost some of its clarity since then, I have not forgotten the lesson.

Enter an environmental stimulus calling me out from inside my head again: I hear the sound of surf. Or I think I do. Is it just my paddle pushing water? The paddles of others? Yes … no … there! It is the sound of surf – gentle, rhythmic surf on the shore of something somewhere near. Wait … it's a sound in my head … it's fainter now … how can it be fainter? I'm confused for a moment more and then the sound is back and it's quiet and subtle and it's regular. Water washing rock.

Then something that at least felt like a miracle unfolded before me. The faintest of shadows appeared. At first I became aware of barely perceivable darkening of the fog's grayness, just a shade or two. But this had happened earlier in the crossing. My mind had painted more than one mirage on the canvas of fog … momentarily conjured boats, ghost mountains, human figures. This could be another cheap fog trick. As I think about it now, I was getting closer to a hidden masterpiece beneath the cloak of another painting or gray-coated canvas. By paddling forward I was applying the gentle rubbing of a solvent-damped cotton ball, dissolving one image to reveal the highlights of another. Here again the cotton ball wiped away a layer of image, coaxing forth the shadow and there it was, a long-lost Renoir.

In a moment I remember precisely, the fog coalesced into a stand of black spruce trees in the center of a rusty granite coast. Thirty feet in front of me, out of nowhere, an island materialized into my world, full of muted greens and browns. The joy I felt in that moment was rare. Part of me laughed, part of me sighed, and a shudder rippled through my body. The beauty of the shapes and colors. The ecstasy of my fears of getting lost, of not having the skills to find my way, leading to this pure and magnificent conclusion. I should not have known, but I *did* know, that this was the island we had targeted. Such a casual occurrence for those more intimate with the sea, such an enormous achievement of the body and spirit for me. What a different experience it would have been in clear weather – the weather I came to this trip desperately hoping for. All of the haunting and revelation and challenge would have been lost to me with the target in sight every stroke of the way.

After a brief victory landing (punctuated with congratulations, reverence for the fog-framed sights, and some self-satisfied silence), we charted a new course and set out under the same conditions for another nearby island to spend the night. We set up camp and relished a supper of freshly harvested mussels, stale bread, and the now traditional cous-cous. Sitting beside a small fire just below tideline, we shared quiet conversation, and watched the gentle ripples of a calm sea as far out as the fog allowed.

The quiet moment of common reflection was visited by the sound of a breath. A solitary porpoise rolled by the island with an easy pace just within fog's reach, no more than 20 feet from where we sat. Its seamless exhale-inhale marked every other surfacing, with just the sound of the round of its back and dorsal fin parting water on each alternate rise to the surface. Moments like this define my favorite sort of church – bring me to my own spirituality with ease and a gentle whisper.

By the following morning, the fog had lifted and we got in some clear weather paddling and full-Technicolor scenery as we worked our way back to what I inappropriately and inaccurately used to refer to as the *real world* – as if the world I'd just been visiting, inside and outside myself, were something totally separate and somehow less legitimate.

When we reached the first fish-in-a-barrel island we'd crossed to and rounded her toward our original shore of departure, I could clearly see the reflection off of our van's windshield. No check of the compass required here. This last paddle took longer than I expected, longer than I wanted, and it began to bore me in sharp contrast to the relative magic of the day before. In the bright, glaring sun, under a clear blue sky, and knowing exactly where I was going and how I was going to get there, interest and fun followed fear out the door. Compared to the journey out, the journey back was like a drive to the corner store for a loaf of bread.

I've paddled a few times a year since that trip. Generally, I've beaten the odds and found fair, clear weather off Maine's coast. On short paddles for recreation, I appreciate this. But on the rare occasions when I go on a land or sea retreat from the perennial busy-ness that I am inclined to complain about, I have a broader, and hard-won, definition of good weather. Now it very well may include fog – as an occasion to sharpen my focus and turn it inward, toward the vast, diverse scenery within me.

Craig Werth is a writer of both words and music. His first "above ground" recording of original songs, Loose Gems, *is available on CD. For his day job, Craig is an education program administrator, teacher, and counselor based at the University of New Hampshire. He and his wife, Liz; son, Ben; and dogs, Sophie and Rose, make their home in New Durham, New Hampshire.*

Jan DeBlieu

In late September, a tropical depression in the Caribbean attracted the alarmed attention of meteorologists at the Cape Hatteras weather station in Buxton. The system had formed off the coast of northern Africa, and it gathered strength at an unusual rate as it moved east toward the Lesser Antilles. Its spinning, counterclockwise winds accelerated, then slowed, then doubled in force, skimming salty moisture from the ocean and tossing it into the clouds. At the center of the storm warm air plunged downward, causing drastic shifts in pressure. Like the iris in an eye, the core widened and narrowed. By September 23 the storm had become Gloria, the largest hurricane ever to develop in the Atlantic Ocean.

On Hatteras, news of Gloria's northward movement was greeted at first with little interest. The summer rentals had begun to empty for the season, and the pace of life had slackened. The air, fresh and slightly damp, was full of the melancholy that signals that the hottest days of summer have passed. It was far too pleasant to dwell on the possibility of a major storm. Besides, Gloria was the third hurricane of the season that forecasters had said might swing our way. The others had not come close.

By Tuesday, September 24, Gloria had become enough of a threat to the Atlantic seaboard to merit comment among my neighbors. The next morning I wandered over to the Island Convenience, a small store owned by Mac and Marilyn Midgett. A sprawling complex by Rodanthe standards, it includes a quick-stop grocery, gas station, garage, crane hoisting service, storage yard for broken-down cars, and a real estate office. It is also the place neighborhood residents cash checks and catch up on gossip. The newspaper I picked up had a small story about Gloria on page one. I glanced at it as I pushed my quarter across the counter toward Mac's sister, Mildred Midgett, a solid island woman who is perpetually calm and pleasant.

"How are you, Mildred?" I asked absently, leafing to the paper's back sections.

"I'm fine, but I'm already tired of people talking about this storm. Seems like that's all anyone can think about this morning. One man already came in and said he was evacuating. He said it wasn't worth waiting until the last minute. I guess we'll have some sort of big storm tomorrow, whether it's a hurricane or not."

"Huh. I didn't realize it was that much of a threat. You think you'd leave if it started coming this way?"

"I haven't left for a storm yet."

"I don't know. If the forecasters said it was going to hit us dead on, I think I'd leave. I don't trust my house to stand up in 130-mile-an-hour winds."

Mildred, one of the kindest souls I had met on Hatteras, looked at me askance. "That house has stood through more storms than you have," she said.

The day was cloudy and warm, but the air felt dry. Back at home, I dropped the paper on the kitchen table and made a pot of coffee. I had no television, no reliable radio, no way to monitor Gloria's progress. Neither could I force myself to concentrate on the work I had scheduled for the day. If Gloria did drift toward Hatteras, I would have only a few hours to decide which of my possessions I most cherished and pack them up. But I was letting myself get rattled; I needed to get down to work. I would feel better if I got down to work.

After an hour of staring out the kitchen window at five gulls that circled and swooped above the myrtle, I walked across the street to see Mike Halminski, a wildlife photographer. He emerged from his darkroom with a marine radio and set it on the back porch.

The announcer reported that Gloria was 680 miles south of Cape Hatteras and moving north at 15 miles an hour. If the storm followed the predicted course, it would make landfall on the cape sometime Thursday night. "Hurricane Gloria is a dangerous hurricane with winds gusting to 150 miles an hour. Residents of the Outer Banks should be aware of its progress. … Windows should be boarded or taped, and objects outside that could serve as missiles in hurricane-force winds should be secured. … The biggest loss of life in hurricanes results not from high winds but from drowning. … Heavy surf already threatens to overwash portions of Highway 12 at Pea Island, the S curves north of Rodanthe, portions of Hatteras Island north of Buxton …"

"Pretty scary," Halminski said.

The clouds had grown thicker, and the air was now heavy and damp. "Maybe I'm imagining it," I said, "but there's a really strange feeling in the air."

Halminski looked south toward the Chicamacomico station. "Maybe I should park my truck on that little hill and go on up into the station. It's stood through a lot of storms."

"If it starts to look bad I'm leaving. It's not worth taking the chance."

Robin Gerald, a local jack-of-all-trades, appeared in the doorway. "Anyone want to buy some pictures to remember this place?"

"Or some oceanfront property?" Halminski asked.

The two friends had moved to Hatteras more than a decade before, when they were in their early twenties and the island was only beginning to be developed. Both loved the violence of the Hatteras weather, but neither had ever experienced a major hurricane.

"She blows through here, my house is gone," Gerald said loudly. "That property over there's one of the lowest points on the island. Your house might be okay, might not." He was enjoying himself.

"It would be something to see a storm like that blow in if you knew for sure you were in a safe place," Halminski said.

"I don't have anywhere to go even if I did evacuate," Gerald said. "Nowhere's safe from them things, nowhere that I can go. Better to stay here and go down thrashing."

My stomach churned as I walked back to the house. There was nothing to be concerned about, not yet. Gerald had a knack for embellishment and I was letting it overpower my common sense. The previous year Hurricane Diana had stalled south of Hatteras for two days and park service rangers had cleared the beaches of tourists under fair skies, even as Diana lost much of her power and turned inland two hundred miles south of Ocracoke. Something similar could happen with Gloria. Above all I wanted to avoid being an alarmist. I got the keys to my pickup and pulled into the line that had started to form at the Island Convenience's gas pumps. Inside Mildred and Marilyn were ringing up purchases with studied efficiency, as if nothing unusual was going on. A balding man I had seen but couldn't place walked in behind me. "I'm getting ready to evacuate," he announced.

"You are?" Mildred asked. She seemed surprised.

"Yes. If it was just me I could take care of myself, but I have to think of mother, you know."

At home I called Wally DeMaurice, a meteorologist I had once talked with about hurricanes and northeasters. Gloria had been declared a Category Five storm, the worst on the scale, with winds of 150 miles an hour or greater. "Looks like your predictions of doom may come true," I said when DeMaurice reached the phone. "But really – is this storm any different from Diana?"

"Oh, very much so. It has the potential to be a real killer. There's no reason to expect it to lose strength, and it will be approaching our area at about 25 miles an hour. That's five times faster than Diana. And one of the complicating factors is that we're in a period of astronomically high tides. We're already running about three feet above normal, which with heavy northeast winds is enough to cause overwashes in several sections of the island. I'm going to send my wife and son off the island tomorrow if things keep looking like they look now. I've got to stay. Get back in touch with me after the storm, if I'm still around." He chuckled grimly.

I hung up with a shaky hand. For the first time I looked hard at the photographs of my family, the porcelain jewelry box on my dresser, the jeans and sweaters in my overflowing closet. Which of these could not be replaced? I had far too many things to take, but how would I whittle down my list of valuables to a manageable size? To calm myself I began gathering notebooks, sorting papers, making mental lists. The framed pictures would have to come off the walls in case the house started shaking – which seemed more than likely in hurricane-force winds. The stereo could be moved to a cabinet in the dining room.

Did I have enough water in jugs for after the storm? I took down a kerosene lantern, filled it, and checked the wick. The electricity could go off at any moment, hurricane or no. Outside, I unlashed the bird feeders I had hung on the clothesline supports, and I piled cinder blocks on top of two doors I had stored on the back porch. Could a hurricane hurl a cinder block through a wall? Maybe, but if the wind reached that strength the house would probably break up.

Nearby I could hear the whirr of saws and the hammering of nails as a cottage owner boarded his windows. I had no plywood, but most of my windows contained small mullions that might withstand the wind. It was barely afternoon, anyway, and I would probably not leave until the next morning, if at all. For something to do I wandered down to the beach. The steel-gray water swelled fully but broke with little force. In recent weeks the beach had steepened. Now it dropped to the water in three steps: a six-inch ledge at the high-tide mark, a thirty-degree incline at the low-tide line, and a final scarp ten yards below that caused incoming waves to break a second time. Beyond that, the bottom had built and flattened as the weaker summer surf carried sand inland from nearby shoals. Nothing appeared the least unusual.

I went home and turned my dilapidated radio to an AM channel which blurred with static. Gloria had moved fifty miles closer and was expected to pick up speed. The Dare County Commissioners advised Hatteras Island residents to prepare for evacuation before sunset. A mandatory evacuation had already been ordered for Ocracoke Island since rough water was expected to suspend ferry operations by midnight. If the storm continued on its predicted course, the Outer Banks might receive ocean surges of up to eighteen feet. The ground beneath my house was only four feet above sea level. An eighteen-foot tide would put the first floor under water.

I had no choice but to leave. Hurrying to the kitchen, I pulled from the cabinets a hand-painted platter that had been a gift from a friend and a pair of delft candlesticks my father had brought me from Holland. In my office I moved a clock, a vase, and an antique microscope away from the windows and stuffed my most important files into boxes to be put in the truck. I considered carrying a few things upstairs to protect them from flooding, but remembered that the roof could possibly come off.

I lowered the storm windows, moved furniture away from outside walls, stuffed a suitcase with clothes, packed a single box of mementos. The rest could be replaced. I had heard that a few windows should be left cracked to relieve sudden, drastic pressure changes as the eye of the hurricane passed over, so I raised two of the storms. The telephone rang with calls from anxious friends: I was leaving, wasn't I? I opened the door to the freezer and looked at my stockpile of food. All of it would be lost if the power went out for days. But if that were all I lost, I would feel exceedingly lucky.

I paused on the front porch long enough to wave to Halminski, who was loading boxes into his truck. "I'm going tonight," he called. "No sense hanging around and taking a chance on the roads." He was not alone. A steady flow of cars, campers, and trucks with trailered boats had begun moving north.

Near 8 o'clock, an hour after dark, I surveyed the rooms a final time to check for items that needed to be secured. The sounds of sawing and hammering had grown louder; probably they would continue well into the night. I glanced briefly at two posters tacked to the kitchen wall and a ceramic pitcher on top of the hutch – they really could be replaced – before breezing through the living room and bedroom. I turned out the lights and locked the front door. As I drove away a feeling of nausea and fear settled firmly in my gut.

*   *   *

I drove only as far as Nags Head that night, bedding down on a friend's floor and making plans to turn inland the next day. By 11 P.M. the pace of the storm had slowed, and it was still five hundred miles south of the cape. I went to sleep feeling calmer and slightly foolish for fleeing so soon.

At daybreak the air was motionless, the sky cast with a textureless layer of cloud. The morning felt ominously empty, like the sudden, heavy silence that precedes an explosion of temper. Every television channel was filled with news about Gloria's move to within four hundred miles of the cape. I called the National Park Service and learned that Highway 12 had not flooded; as I had feared, I had been spooked into leaving too early.

As I drove west, past motels with "No Vacancy" signs in Columbia and Plymouth, past crowded emergency shelters in Williamston, Gloria neared shore and began to threaten Morehead City, fifty miles southwest of Ocracoke. As I arrived at a friend's house in Kinston and unloaded my gear, the hurricane turned north, directly toward Hatteras. The wind rose. The heavy rains expected all day began just after dark. I sagged into bed at 10:30 with Gloria ninety miles off the cape and moving north at 25 miles an hour.

If the storm traveled up Pamlico Sound, Hatteras Island would be to its east. The greatest winds and most dangerous storm surges occur in the northeast quadrant of a hurricane, where the forward motion of the storm boosts the power of the gusts. If the wind speed alone was 120 miles an hour and the storm moved north at 25 miles an hour, the combined winds would be 145 – strong enough to destroy most buildings. Even if it passed east of the island, the damage could be significant. Maybe, I thought, maybe it will still stall and go out to sea. The branches of two red maples scraped the roof as I fell asleep.

At 2:30 I woke up, startled by the quietness. The wind had quit, and my head felt stuffed with cotton. I crept downstairs to the living room and turned on the television. A map of eastern North Carolina flashed on the screen. "And as we reported an hour ago, Gloria did make landfall at Buxton on Hatteras Island about 1:15 and is making her way up the coast," the weatherman said. "Reconnaissance flights show that she has already passed through the town of Avon, and the eye is about ten miles north of there at this time. It appears that the serious damage from the storm will be limited to the Outer Banks. So most of us in eastern North Carolina have a lot to be thankful for this evening."

Ten miles north of Avon! Five miles south of Rodanthe! Right now the winds would be blowing hard out of the east. The house would be shaking; dishes might be crashing out of cabinets. Gloria had been downgraded to a low Category Four hurricane, which meant gusts of only 130. A difference of 20 miles an hour did not strike me, just then, as significant. At least the storm had hit near low tide; the strong lunar pull meant that tides would be unusually low as well as unusually high. Still, the ocean would be splashing over the dunes at the S curves and flowing down Highway 12, which would become a riverbed. Water would be lapping at my front door, my back door, maybe trickling into cracks. As the eye passed over, the air would grow still for perhaps twenty minutes. Then a hard west wind would slam the house, bringing a flood from the sound. I should have boarded the windows. I should have boxed up the ceramic pitcher.

I am standing in the kitchen. The wind has ripped my favorite posters off the wall. A spray of rain is blowing through a shattered window, and the water in the house is already six inches deep. Two plastic cups bob next to the hutch, which is lying on its side. An avalanche of broken glass spills from its open door. The flood is rising fast, but it hasn't reached the paintings I piled on top of the pub table in the dining room. Maybe it won't. The table's no great loss; it needed to be refinished, anyway. . . . I am in my bedroom shaking my head at the twisted frame of my iron bed. A minute ago the dresser fell over and bent the footboard so badly it can never be straightened. The house is still vibrating, and it looks like the two northeast windows will be broken out by waves any time. Upstairs the roof is leaking; water has begun to drip down the stairs.

★   ★   ★

The light the next day was a splendid yellow glaze that ricocheted from puddles and stabbed at my chafed, swollen eyes. The sky was cloudless, the weather unseasonably warm. By the time I reached Nags Head, the day had attained a peacefulness that only heightened the numb sensation produced by my lack of sleep. The waves that had swamped the causeway between Manteo and Nags Head drained off before noon. By 1 o'clock a line had formed at Whalebone Junction, the crossroads in south Nags Head where Highway 12 forks to the south. Some Hatteras residents had been able to return home by boat but the rest of us were told we would have to wait until the highway was reopened at 6:00.

The information available about conditions on the island was sketchy and certain details only heightened my worry. Most of Hatteras had flooded; there was talk, in fact, that a new inlet had been cut through. Rumors circulated that three houses had burned in electrical fires. Other rumors reported that damages were surprisingly light. Telephone calls to the Buxton weather station and the Dare County sheriff's office in Buxton brought news that the wind speed had reach only 87 miles an hour on the island and that no one had been killed. Nevertheless, the force of the winds that preceded the storm had pushed most of the water in Pamlico Sound northward into the mainland's rivers and creeks. The harbors at Hatteras and Avon had been sucked dry; then, after the eye of the storm passed, the water had gushed back in a twelve-foot wave. Many homes had been badly flooded; a few had collapsed.

A radio station in Kinston reported that two houses in Rodanthe had exploded. My heart lodged firmly in my throat.

Just before 6:00 – forty-five minutes before dark – the barricades were moved aside and a mile-long string of traffic unleashed. Cars and trucks crowded behind recreational vehicles that slowed for four-inch-deep puddles. I drove three miles, then stopped dead behind an Airstream trailer. Five minutes later, the line of traffic moved on.

As I began the descent from the bridge I could see water lapping into the ridge of shrubs along the sound. The six-yard-wide beach in front of the shrubs was submerged. Farther south a line of telephone poles keeled badly to the east and wire tangled on the ground. Thick swirls of eelgrass and rushes marked where the sound had crashed across the road and into the fields, almost to the primary dunes. Patches of mud, rippled in a pattern left by waves, covered the pavement. To my surprise, the tall, stately dunes on Pea Island appeared unscathed.

Bulldozers had scraped sand off the road at the S curves and piled it into six-foot mounds, next to chunks of wood and piles of rush stems. I braked briefly for the turns and accelerated in a burst. The roof of my house was still there and still shingled. I pulled carefully into the driveway – numb, anxious, afraid to go inside.

Flounder, pike, and croaker carcasses were strewn among the reeds and the standing water smelled of marsh and mud. A wave had deposited a line of eelgrass on the top step, but the front porch was dry. Still aware of the traffic streaking by, I unlocked the door in the diminishing light, sucked in my breath, kicked off my sandals, and stepped into the living room. The rug was dry. I shined my flashlight on the windows, across the sofa to the stairs and back into the kitchen. Except for a small puddle in the kitchen that had blown under the back door, the entire downstairs was dry. The second story was also undamaged. This cannot be, I thought, letting my gaze float around the rooms, to the paintings on the pub table, the posters in the kitchen, the ceramic pitcher. I lit the kerosene lamp and sat down, slowly, in the kitchen. The last light of evening I had come to love so well seeped through salt-sprayed windows.

★   ★   ★

The next morning, when finally I pulled myself out of bed, the grass in my yard was an ashen gray from salt and mud. Traffic cruised slowly past the house as the first groups of sightseers trickled into town. Most declared Rodanthe a disappointment – nothing to see except residents drying out clothes and carpets – but in Avon the damage was more sensational. At least two houses lay in shreds.

The towns of the cape began to buzz with the camaraderie and good will that accompany disasters. Normally taciturn neighbors toured each other's houses, inspecting the damage and trading tales. People whose homes had not been flooded made up spare beds for the less fortunate, then pooled their foodstuffs and cleaning supplies. My house had been one of the few ground-level structures to escape flooding as Gloria pushed four feet of water through town. A fish house on the creek near my backyard marsh had exploded, its walls apparently pushed out by changes in pressure. Beyond it lay a swath of reed stems and trash thrown to the northeast – directly toward my house – by the surge from the sound. In the old village of Avon, two hundred houses had flooded, some by as much as seven feet, and the reported damages would exceed one million dollars. But the towns of Hatteras had stood, had even suffered remarkably little damage. Like several of my neighbors, I began to wish I had stayed through the storm.

Meals became unusually festive as freezers defrosted and stocks of food thawed. Saturday night Halminski boiled ten pounds of shrimp, and Debbie Bell grilled eight pounds of steak raised at her father's farm on the mainland. In the absence of normal life, people organized their days around meals. Only minimal cleanup work could be done without electricity to pump water, and even when the power was restored, many wells would be salty from the tide and polluted from overflowing septic tanks.

Stories began circulating of people who had stayed through the storm, what they had witnessed, and how they had reacted. In Avon, where wind gauges had recorded gusts of more than 100 miles an hour, residents retreated to the second stories of their houses as water poured into their living rooms and dens. Many of the oldest houses in town had been bolted to their foundations after the hurricanes of 1933 and 1944 had floated them to the beach. As Gloria pushed water from the sound through the village, a few residents cracked open their doors to allow it to flow through their houses rather than splinter the frames.

Rachel Austin pried loose two floorboards in her living room to prevent the flood from pushing up her entire first floor. As the sound tide swept through their front yard and toward the swaybacked house where the Austins had lived for forty years, the seventy-two-year-old woman and her husband, Willie, began piling up their furniture and appliances. Within ten minutes after water began gushing through the floor it had crested the window sills, turning Rachel's flowered wallpaper and yellow curtains a muddy gray. The refrigerator toppled over and the stove twisted from its pipe. A mantel fell out from the wall. But the house was one of the oldest residences on the Outer Banks. Assuming it would stand through one more storm, they retired for the evening in their second-story bedroom. All night they could hear water slopping against their furniture. They slept fitfully, but were content to be dry and warm. The next morning they went downstairs to find the kitchen blown off the house.

Again and again I heard people relate tales of stepping out into the eye of the storm and seeing stars, of walking to a neighbor's house in the worst of the wind, of drifting off to sleep and waking disappointed to find Gloria past. A few admitted twinges of anxiety after the sound flooded the island. Only once did I hear a resident express unbridled fright.

Brad Nash has yellow-white hair and a face so tan his blue eyes seem to shine through it like those in a jack-o'-lantern. A crabber and furniture builder who lived with his parents in Avon, he had resided on Hatteras full-time for seven years. As Gloria moved up the coast, he dismissed his parents' pleas to evacuate and settled into the third floor of his house with his dog and two cats. The fourteen-year-old structure sat on three-foot pilings on a canal near the sound.

Nash had tracked Gloria as it moved up the coast and had noticed it was losing strength. As dusk approached and the winds rose, he tuned his maritime radio to the Cape Hatteras station and positioned himself in the living area at the southeast corner of the house. Nearby he had a wind gauge, a telephone, a life preserver, and an open notebook.

"At some point I decided I needed to keep a journal, if only to keep myself sane. I'm not sure when it became clear to me that the storm was actually going to hit. But by seven-thirty or eight I knew I was on Hatteras for good, that there was no getting off."

Nash's notes began at 8 P.M.

> *I feel very much alone. House shaking, pets okay.*

"It occurred to me about this time," Nash said later, "that the buildings around me might pose a big threat. I wasn't worried about this house blowing apart on its own. It's too solid. But there's a house next door on stilts, and I began thinking that its windows might blow out and it might fall over, like a sprung umbrella."

Periodically Nash ventured outside, where he used a large floodlight to watch the water level drop in the sound. By 11:00 the canal beside his house was empty. He remembered that his neighbor had moored a forty-five-foot fishing boat on the far side of the canal. The thought suddenly made his stomach flip. If the boat broke from its mooring after Gloria's eye passed, it would probably ram his house.

The winds increased until Nash could no longer open the east-facing door to a third-story deck.

> *11:30 – House rumbling and shaking bad.*
> *11:50 – Something crashed and broke downstairs. Winds steady at 100+.*
> *Much wind noise – whistling and shrieking.*

"At one point I jammed tissues in my ears because I couldn't stand the noise. It was very shrill. About this time too, an ash tray jumped across a desk and fell on the floor. That's how bad the house was vibrating. It would move considerably; it was like being on board a ship."

> *1:12 – Ears starting to pop. Must yawn to help.*
> *1:35 – Eye here, with winds at 10 mph. Seems dead calm. Barometer at 27.8.*
> *1:55 – Eye gone. Winds west at 40. Very west. Still bone dry outside.*
> *2:24 – 100+ west winds.*
> *2:56 – Strongest winds so far. House moving badly.*
> *3:22 – Phone dead. House being blasted.*

Nash's journal did not make note of what time the sound tide rushed back in from the north. By then, however, he had opened the east-facing door to relieve changes in pressure and had gone outside to survey his immediate surroundings with the floodlight. He watched as a twelve- to fourteen-foot wave approached, lifting debris to its crest and slinging it forward.

"Everything started bobbing and dancing. There was debris all over the place and the water was just sloshing violently. I had some piles of juniper six inches wide and sixteen feet long; they were flying around like Fritos. Waves started hitting the upstairs window.

"The thing that worried me the most was the big boat across the canal. It was straining at its ropes; I thought it had gotten loose. It would pull toward me during a lull, and then a gust would get it and flip it back away from me, like a slingshot. It danced around like crazy, like the tail on a kite. Sometimes I could barely see it, it was moving so fast. And then it would whip toward me again.

"It was about this time that I put on the life preserver."

Around 3:40 Nash crawled out the eastern door, digging his fingers in between the planks on the deck. He could hear bangs and thumps coming from the sound side of the house, but without his floodlight he could not tell if the structure was being damaged. He wore a pair of goggles to protect his eyes. Slowly he slid his head and shoulders around the corner of the house to the west, bracing himself for the impact of Gloria's gusts. The wind caught him in the chest and threw him against the deck railing. He crawled back to safety, but not before he had seen that waves were tossing the fishing boat very close to the house.

> 3:44 – Big boat hitting house. Wind won't die. Can hear lumber cracking
> and breaking. House might go down.
> 4:15 – Helpless. Wind won't stop. House can't stand the damage.
> I'll have a Dr. Pepper and a cigarette.
> 4:39 – Wind down some. It'll be daybreak and nice weather soon.
> 4:40 – It will subside.

Before dawn Nash realized the fishing boat had rammed into a pile of lumber and lodged several yards from the house. By 5:00 the wind had dropped to between 70 and 80 and the sound had begun to recede. Three feet of water still churned through his yard. Two lower-story windows had blown out, and water had washed into his shop on the first floor. But the building was intact.

"At that point," Nash said, "I kissed my pets, I went downstairs, I got on my very wet mattress, and I went to sleep."

Excerpted from "Hurricane," a chapter in Hatteras Journal. *Used by kind permission of the author and Fulcrum Publishing, Golden, Colorado.*

Jan DeBlieu is an author and essayist who lives on the storm-lashed Outer Banks of North Carolina. Much of her writing examines the relationships between people and the landscapes in which they live. Her books include Hatteras Journal, *from which this essay has been taken;* Meant to Be Wild: The Struggle to Save Endangered Species through Captive Breeding; *and most recently,* Wind: How the Flow of Air Has Shaped Life, Myth, and the Land *(Houghton Mifflin, 1998).*

Aristotle's Rainbow

...and it's spring when the world is puddle-wonderful...
e. e. cummings, from Chansons Innocentes

Catherine Buni

PUDDLES AREN'T what they used to be. This is what I was thinking as I slogged down the wet street, arm crossed over my nose and mouth to mask the stench of sewage wafting from a pool of rain filling a depressed corner in Cambridge. It had poured what felt like all spring – June broke rain history – and puddles flooded every last one of winter's potholes, and more than a few basements. But puddles aren't they used to be. If they were, I thought, awash in a moment of parental predilection for nostalgia, kids would be playing in this one. Floating boats. Splashing. Stomping.

Soaking wet and sitting in a circle with other puddle-loving children. Trailing wrinkled fingers to stir up mini wakes and whirlpools. Letting the warm spring rain rinse away winter's dry skin of stale indoor air.

I can still see my two brothers on the top step of our front porch two towns west of Cambridge, their arms outstretched, palms to the clouds, the bony ridges of their shoulder blades outlined in dripping T-shirts. By turn, they would dare each other to step into the storm. One step, two, three, they'd race down and up, touching down quick as first-time fire walkers. The rain drummed, and my brothers laughed, their skinny wet arms lit up by lightning.

Across the street, the Cleland's two pear trees danced, their waving branches flinging white petals into the wind. The telephone wires, all silver and shimmer, swung wildly overhead. Swagged between utility poles, the wires shook and shimmied down the street to where they hung above the intersection at my best friend's house.

There, at the crossroads, pulsing in lightning strobe, glowed the puddle. And there we were, deep in it. Mind you, swimming ordinarily involved Mom, sweaty vinyl car seats, and interminable 15-minute "rest periods" during which the grown-ups breast-stroked back and forth, back and forth in the deep end while we purple-lipped kids shivered in damp and faded towels. But when it rained a warm spring rain, aquatic abandon was ours, as easy as splashing down the front steps and into the street.

The puddle was huge. I always wanted it to flood the entire intersection. Five roads converged there, creating a concrete bowl the size of a baseball diamond. On dry days, we'd pedal around the perimeter, glittery handlebar fringe flapping, and take turns jumping our bikes over the lip of the asphalt on the corner of Newell and Meadowbrook, retreating to the grassy sidelines when cars motored past. On rainy days, the water and I seemed to have no place else to go and rushed to fill it in.

My bare feet would hit the road, bathwater warm and gritty with dirt washed from kid-worn lawns. I would run through lightning and thunder to the puddle and plop down in its murky, rib-deep water. I remember my skin feeling soft and slippery and cool. Later, dressed again in dry clothes, my arms held that sweet scent of rain for what felt like hours, and I'd lie on the living room floor and rest my head on crossed arms to breath it in.

Aristotle believed the heavenly, earthly redolence of rain was carried on rainbows. "The reason for the sweet smell," he wrote, "is the same as the earth smell, for whatever grows out of it, is sweet scented to begin with." On those rainy days when the puddle on our suburban street turned into a pond just big enough for a child to play in, I knew I came from the earth, just like the rain. I knew I smelled sweet, like Aristotle's rainbow.

Summers, my parents would pack up the car and follow the roads north. In the woods, I discovered rain falls in symphony, with wind playing bold crescendos on leaves and branches and swollen streams hitting the high notes. Pine duff mutes.

Cool drops bounce *staccato* on new leaves. Even after the rain stops, the forest continues to hum a clear melody, with raindrops falling like shining half notes through bars of sunlight newly drawn.

From what I understand, most American children today – two-thirds, I'm told – grow up where the rain falls in large measure on asphalt and concrete: roads and sidewalks and parking lots. In cities and suburbs, the rain drums monotonic on a paved path to the storm drains, and carries with it all manner of unearthliness. When I read the news that this June's deluge had swamped much of Boston in sewage, I was glad I was no longer a kid. Would I have played in the puddle if I had known that in the United States, more than 38 million acres lie buried under roads and parking lots slick with gasoline, motor oil, worn out tire tread, antifreeze? That half of the 70-or-so million gallons of rain that fell onto the United States today was turned into a fetid cocktail of rainwater mixed with not only this road filth but lawn fertilizers, herbicides, pesticides, household detergents, and, in some cases, the contents of our toilets? That this befouled rainwater – runoff, to specialists – accounts for more than 60 percent of America's water pollution? This is what I was thinking as I walked past a puddle this June.

Ready to turn for home, I looked down at my son, Ben, asleep in his stroller, and watched for signs that his newborn nose could yet distinguish sweet from foul. But he slept contentedly, the rain drumming softly on the stroller's vinyl rain cover. The stench gradually faded and I uncovered my nose, breathing through my mouth until I was certain the smell had gone. I walked to the next corner, past a blue painted plaque on a high wooden fence surrounding the house where e. e. cummings had been born 105 years ago. Perhaps the young Edward Estlin had played here once, when it was spring and the world was puddle-wonderful. Squinting through the drops trickling from my hood, I looked ahead, believing the perfect puddle sat somewhere still in warm spring rain.

Catherine Buni, former editor and publisher of AMC Outdoors, *writes from her homes in Somerville, Massachusetts, and Locke Mills, Maine, where she lives with her husband Bill, and her son, Ben. Her work has been published in* Outdoor Explorer, Outside's Family Adventures, *and* Backpacker, *among others. She is currently at work on a book about women explorers.*

Eric Pinder

No one foresees the coming of glaciers. No one wakens to the sight of four fresh inches of snow on a cold, sunny Monday morning and says, "This is the one, the storm that will last a million lifetimes." There's only one way to know a glacier is coming, and that's to see the wall of ice, to guess where it will flow, and to get out of the way.

On December nights in the village in the mountains where my grandmother once lived, tree branches slick with ice wrap around the street lamps like long, sparkling prisms. The trees resemble glass, pure and light, intricate and brittle. Electric light pulses around them, a bright gleam of warmth filtered through the shadowed, woody branches deep in ice. Light disperses into the darkness of early evening.

It has yet to snow. Leftover November leaves, dry and cracked, rustle in the dead grass or blow with the breezes, chasing their shadows around the trunks of trees. A branch, heavy with ice, sags to eye level. In summer, free from the burden of snow and ice, it springs many feet higher, a safe perch for birds and squirrels.

By night the tree looks a delicate crystal sculpture, a Christmas ornament planted in the town park. Its branches hold still in the wind, and the rod of a street lamp rises through them, burning yellow at the top. The tree sits inside this cold glass like an exhibit of summer. A few leaves stick to its top, hard and heavy, the rough, grooved bark smoothed over. By day, the tree is slippery, dripping with warm, wet ice.

When snow finally does fall, paths blur and fade; the pothole-ridden road to Roaring Brook fills and vanishes. A boot makes a crisp, heavy footprint in the first inch of snow, but soon withers, fades away like a ghost. Younger snow fills it in, leaving in time the palest outline of a foot, then only a small depression, then nothing but a fresh white plain, all signs of human passage erased.

The three-pronged tracks of rabbits dash and dart under the trees, long hours after the animals themselves have gone. To discover the habits of rabbits in the morning, follow the tracks.

A footprint, while it lasts, dents the whiteness, as if some entity of its maker still hovers in that place. While new snow fills it in, it does no good to dig it out, or to renew the footprint. Snow is only patience and water. It outlasts the most dedicated shoveller, but yields at last to spring.

But some winters refuse to yield. There were times – many times during the ice ages of the past three million years – when the snow renewed itself faster than it could be melted by the sun. The relatively recent Wisconsin glaciation pushed the Laurentide Ice Cap over much of North America, covering its greatest expanse 18,000 years ago. Today the ice age is waning; perhaps it's over. But what if it is not? What if the ice of this year's winter were to harden on our roads, to stick there despite all efforts of salt and plow, strengthened by snows that fall and keep falling? Suppose that glossy tree on a street corner stays icy into July, like the glaciers on the northern slopes of mountains? The clear ice swells and darkens until only a dim, distorted shadow of tree peeks out through a frozen husk. Sleet clings to the street lamp, thickening. It emits an ebbing trickle of light.

In the woods, bears stumble out of their dens, sleepy and hungry, and flee south in search of food. Instinct triggers a thought in the brains of birds, a need to fly north out of the warmth of Florida. The program of migration is etched into their minds, and they follow it back to higher latitudes, only to find a place still hard and white with ice. Warily they circle overhead, confused. Instinct has gone wrong; cold reason sends them away, back to warmer climes.

Snow piles on the streets of towns, burying them more and more as April edges into May. The weather becomes front page news. The Sunday *New York Times* claims it is the harshest winter on record, a fact that is obvious to everyone. For a week in late May, the sun shines. Some of the snow melts, but not enough. It refreezes as a slick layer of ice. In time, the snow level rises. Cars disappear underground. In June, the highway department abandons the roads. A press release explains that plows are able to clear off layers of fresh snow, but cannot attack the thick ice underneath. The National Guard is called in, and the first of what soon becomes a dozen towns is evacuated by helicopter. Civilization retreats south.

Houses soon sink underground, one floor at a time, for the surface layer is a rising field of hard ice. Ceilings collapse, and scattered cracks ring like gunshots all around town as mounds of ice bring roofs careening down into basements, there to lie buried by snow. The trees fail to sprout new leaves and die. Grasses and shrubs, denied sunlight for a year, also die, never to return. Bright orange jackets freeze in deserted houses invaded by snow. No one from rural counties goes hunting next December; there is nothing to hunt, no one to go hunting. The roof of a hospital on Somerset Street holds up briefly but the building itself is lost under ice; an antenna protrudes from the whiteness, like a wand of grass in a field. Soon the last roof caves in. The smokestacks at the paper mill in Millinocket, Maine, expand and crumble, plugged with ice. All traces of the once-bustling downtown district of town are gone. Farther north, the craggy peaks of mountains turn to hard white lumps in a monotonous world of white. The glacier has returned.

Continental glaciers swept repeatedly over North America during the Pleistocene Epoch, two million years ago, not long after the ancestors of our species stood erect for the first time. These pre-humans were a stunted race by our standards, undernourished yet ill-equipped to hunt food, with cramped brains that spared little room for thought. But unlike their cousins, the apes, their brains continued to grow, and straight spines freed their hands from the burden of locomotion. This was on warm plains of Africa, long sundered from North America, still rapidly pulling away from the New World across the Atlantic.

The continental glacier sucked water from the northern seas and froze it, dropping worldwide ocean levels a maximum of 400 feet. It thrust a great sheet of ice south over North America. The land that is now Maine, New Hampshire, Vermont, and New York did not escape, but neither did it suffer a slow death, buried gradually under newer and newer snows. It was ploughed down, destroyed, scoured clean by the onslaught of ice. No houses or human dwellings of any sort interrupted the vast swath of coniferous forest that covered the cold stones, for people did not exist yet. But there were trees – thick forests lost to a long, deadly winter.

Caribou lived in those woods, and savage bears, and strange mammals never seen by human eyes. If they looked north they saw a tongue of ice, hundreds of feet thick, inching closer month by month, snapping the trunks of trees under its weight. In spurts, spurred on by heavy snowfalls on its northern flank in Canada, sections of the ice giant shifted their weight and oozed softer layers of ice down over older, harder layers. In the middle of the early-Ice Age forest, in a land that would much later become the village of Millinocket the view of this approaching monster was blocked by a heavily forested mountain, tall and smooth, much like the Great Smokies of today; it did not yet have a name. Caribou watched the ice coming, felt an ominous chill in the wind, and left.

As the ice sheet advanced slowly, year by year, it struck the mountain, surged briefly upward, but fell back. Instead, the ice seeped around the sides, crushing the forests to the south but leaving the high peaks untouched – for now. The advancing bulk of the continental glacier swept south to the coast, dipping its icy paws in the relatively warm waters of the Atlantic.

Smaller valley glaciers had already formed on the slopes of mountains. Frost pried loose boulders and crumbled each mountain's walls. Ice began to carve out the basins called cirques, but its work was interrupted. The continental glacier swelled; the level of ice rose through the millennia, creeping up the side of the mountain and onto the alpine tablelands, and then at last to the highest peaks. The summits, and the entire edge of the North American continent, sagged under the weight of mile-high hard ice.

Every hundred thousand years or so, the sun pushed back the ice, warming the exposed rocks. It let soil gather on bedrock. Plants began to bloom. The shade of trees returned, birds sang in the branches, and animals much like squirrels jumped from tree to tree. Somewhere, thousands of miles distant, a half-human cut open its thumb on a jagged chip of slate and moments later invented the knife. Much later, the sun would again turn a cold shoulder to the Earth, and ice would creep down from the poles.

Snow, water, ice, and wind are the four elements of winter. Three of these entities share the same ingredients yet scarcely resemble each other. They shape the land in different ways: ice does the digging and splitting, water carries, snow insulates rocks and trees against the fierce winds. Wind, the fourth element, shapes ice, swirls snow into great mounds, stirs the still water on the surface of ponds. Wind carries warmth and wind carries cold; it directs where the ice will go. When it wishes, it pushes Arctic air masses deep into the south to nullify the warmth of the sun. Ice sheets bury a continent; a hundred thousand years later wind breathes warm air on the glaciers, sends them scurrying back to the poles.

Snow has eased off in recent years. I've missed it. Once it was possible to hope for a white Thanksgiving and not be disappointed; a white Christmas was guaranteed. Now these things are not so certain. May surprises, such as a foot of sticky snow, are all but unheard of. The Earth has warmed, is warming still, and the memories of glaciers fade off in the distance like the ice cap over Greenland.

The average surface temperature of planet Earth is currently 59 degrees Fahrenheit, thanks in large part to the natural "greenhouse" effect – the emitting of heat by so-called greenhouse gasses in the atmosphere, such as carbon dioxide and water vapor. Without it, the average temperature would plummet to nearly zero degrees Fahrenheit, a permanent, planetary deep freeze.

The increasing number of newspaper headlines about global warming reflect fears that the greenhouse effect may someday run amok, boosted by a human-induced increase in carbon dioxide, heating the globe to intolerable levels. But the Earth's climate has swung from hot to cold many times in the past. In the middle of the last glacial epoch, the average global temperature sank to only 49 degrees Fahrenheit, 10 degrees lower than today. That's all it takes to trigger an Ice Age.

Climatologists have also estimated that temperatures during interglacial warming periods are sometimes five or more degrees *higher* on average than today.

Slight variations in the tilt of Earth's axis, a 93,000-year fluctuation in the eccentricity of the planet's orbit around the sun, and the fact that Earth spins like a wobbly top around its axis on a 25,000-year cycle all play a role in modifying the climate over long stretches of time. So who knows what the future may bring?

Last year, for months, there was nothing to indicate that winter had arrived – just dead grass leaning over a thin, dusty snow. It was February before the hills looked like proper winter, before the trees stood hunched under heavy shoulders of white.

Inside my grandmother's house it is artificially warm; the air hums with the sound of heat pumped through pipes. Outside the window it's black, but a fat bush scrapes against the frosted glass, and on it rests a fresh white coat. It's 4 A.M. I go out to walk in the first real snowfall of the year.

There's a moon somewhere in the fog, but it can't be seen. Up close the air is clear. I can see the slope of the ground, see the dark arms of spruce trees holding up blankets of snow four inches thick. It's too dark to see the sheets of snow still falling, but I can feel them drift across my face, fall on my shoulders and slide down the fabric of my coat. It sounds like a dry snow, light and small. The rippling of creek waters is strong and clear; in daylight this sound would hardly be noticed.

The land is alive in a soft light that comes from everywhere and nowhere. The sky is a grey ceiling, solid and motionless. Sometimes in such a fog the moon shrinks to a pale blur, no longer round, like a weak light burning in deep water.

A bright yellow glow ignites suddenly on a hilltop. Shortly after I hear the pounding of a car's motor – an old car, struggling and coughing. The sound draws nearer, and headlights shine across the ground. It is a sudden, blinding explosion of light – for a moment, the air is filled with a billion floating drops of snow. A billion snowflakes are twisting and spinning in the wind; then the car goes past and all is dark again. Snow falls, silent and invisible.

Eric Pinder is a freelance journalist and writer-in-residence at The Mount Washington Observatory. His first book, Life at the Top, *describes his ongoing experiences as a weather observer on Mount Washington. He has a degree in journalism from Hampshire College and has written for several publications. He lives in Berlin, New Hampshire. His essay "Ice" is an excerpt from a book-in-progress about people and nature.*

A PERFECT BEGINNING

Dave Thurlow

EACH YEAR winter manages to sneak up on me and my nonagricultural lifestyle. This is somewhat embarrassing to admit because I'm a meteorologist (which is also somewhat embarrassing to admit) – it's my job to watch New England's weather.

So, what's my excuse? Why do I spend the month of December scraping my windshield with a plastic cassette cover and tiptoeing through snow banks like a lunatic because my Sorels have yet to migrate out from the back of the closet? You would think that a meteorologist, of all people, would be there on the front steps, shovel in hand, wrapped in a cocoon of Gore-Tex and down, staring skyward for a glimpse of the season's first snowflake.

For me, and many of my fellow winter weather worshippers, the anticipation of winter actually supersedes winter itself. I get so caught up in the drama of winter's first snow storm that I just don't think about snow tires or windshield fluid or even where I buried my mittens.

If waking up to a fresh snowfall doesn't bring some sort of primal combination of comfort and wonder, then it's really time to start thinking about a different latitude. Here in New England you can't look at snow as the stuff that slows down the commute or cancels the meeting, because if you get into that rut you'll be miserable for a third of the year. Remember that for an all-too-short part of our lives – that period we refer to as childhood – a winter snowstorm provides perhaps the single most joyous occasion imaginable: a no-school day.

I remember this particular form of drama unfolding with the evening forecast, and the TV weathermen (they were all men back in the dark recesses of the 1960s) could play it for all it was worth. Back then there were no computer-enhanced radar and satellite pictures, or earth-track-whatever graphic gizmos to play with. Instead, a TV weather map was actually drawn on the blackboard with isobars and fronts and lows and highs and other such things meteorological. Like reading, it summoned the imagination, and it was this excited imagination that kept my junior high brain racing long after the body, and the parents, said it was time for bed.

I don't know what first creeps into the 6 A.M. consciousness of a dreary school-bound 12-year-old on a normal day, but on a not-so-normal, potential-no-school day, there's an influx of information that can size up the meteorological situation before the head rises from the pillow. The sound of traffic provided the morning's first weather observation.

First of all, was there any sound at all? Were the whines and whirs of tires muffled by snow? On only one day, in February of 1969, do I remember waking up to the wonderful silence of more snow than could be plowed. It was a week before I saw a school bus.

The speed of traffic also gave clues, as could the sound of splashing puddles, that dreaded sound of water in its liquid form that surely meant a change to rain, and a waste of perfectly good precipitation. The best clue, of course, was the snowplow. The slow-moving muffled sound of a plow pushing deep snow was what I wanted to hear. If a plow whizzed by, scraping its blade against the pavement, leaving nothing in its wake, then the school buses were soon to follow.

In the town where I grew up, the fire whistle blew at 6:45 if school was canceled. On such a day, the sound heard in most houses at 6:46 was the sound of kids like me jumping out of bed. The memories of such moments are so strong that to this day I can't imagine a casual acceptance of a fresh coating of snow, or less than a few moments of pure amazement over what the atmosphere can produce.

I spent time this past fall combing the New Hampshire hills for woolly bear caterpillars. I found two. I was hoping to conduct some scientific research on a well-known bit of winter weather folklore that ascribes the woolly bear with a prognosticative proficiency beyond that of your average larvae. This is how the story goes: If the woolly bear's coat consists of a narrow brown band sandwiched between two wide black bands of fuzz, then a cold and snowy winter awaits. If the brown band is wide and the two black bands skinny, you can leave the snow shovels in the basement. The problem with my not-so-significant sample of two caterpillars was that one little fella (just assuming) possessed the former characteristics, the other the latter.

The fact is, the woolly bear's autumn sartorial splendor has about as much to do with the severity of the upcoming winter as it has to do with the price of lawn furniture. And this has been proven by real scientists, not only by me. It is amazing that in spite of their relative inaccuracy, winter weather proverbs endure. The squirrel and its acorns, the goose bone and its spots, even the groundhog and its own holiday, have all quite miserably failed any scientific scrutiny hurled their way. Yet, the folklore survives.

While woolly bears change coats, people respond to winter by creating myths, legend, and folklore, I guess in some way supplying a sort of psychological edge. It's optimism and control we yearn for as the days become frightfully short and dark, the trees bare. With the end seemingly near, we'll take proverbs, the *Old Farmer's Almanac,* and woolly bears to put our minds at ease.

With my woolly bear survey run amok, I wondered if my desire to look into the future might be better served by observing my fellow humans' behaviors, rather than by crawling around in the forest, measuring the stripes on caterpillars and counting acorns. In October, I learned that not a single snowblower could be found in stores from Boston to Washington, D.C. Sold out! And in upstate New York, bags of rock salt were flying off the store shelves at a pace never seen before. Also, just down the street, my neighbors have stacked a dozen cords of firewood, twice as much as last year.

It's mid-November as I write, and so far the fall has been extremely warm and dry. An elderly friend says the snow won't fall until the ponds freeze. I asked when that would be and she said "Oh, after the swamps are full." So, according to this bit of wisdom, we need a warm rain then a dry cold spell before the white stuff begins to pile up and the ultimate source of all the earth's energy, the sun, seems to go into hiding.

The winter sun delivers a less concentrated beam of energy, for a shorter period of time each day. In winter, the sun's lack of enthusiasm means that food is scarce, that water is frozen, that shelter is needed, and that life is tough.

It's no surprise that many of our winter holidays are steeped in traditions that involve lots of food. Thanksgiving, Christmas, Chanukah, Candlemas (which has evolved into Groundhog Day) – all are associated with feasting. In spite of the shortages, food is set aside for these occasions to remind us that life goes on, to provide that needed shot of optimism.

Huge chunks of the globe don't even have winter. This begs the question, What is winter? Ecologists define a winter climate as one that includes three months of average temperature below 30 degrees Fahrenheit, and two months of snow-covered ground. A line across the country separating areas with and without these criteria runs roughly on a sweeping arc from Philadelphia to Denver to Seattle. To the north of this line, true winter; to the south, fake winter. Coincidentally, or maybe not, this line also marks the southernmost end of the range of spruce trees, truly winter's indicator species.

There is a climate boundary along this line as well. It marks the average southern terminus of what meteorologists call Arctic air masses, huge pools of heavy cold air that spill out of central Canada, spreading like poured molasses, undercutting the warm southern air at precise, clashing battle zones known as fronts. Forgive the military analogies, but it is the confrontation of air masses of conflicting density and moisture content that produces the atmospheric dissonance we call storms. It is no coincidence that the bulk of this continent's winter storms cruise this very zone, lumbering their way from west to east.

All living things cope with winter in one of two ways; they either hang around and deal with it, or they leave. It's that simple – fight or flight. Winter ecologists call these two coping mechanisms tolerance and avoidance. Now, don't look at this as a conscious decision that every individual member of every species makes every year around Labor Day. Making decisions is not something you would associate with, oh, say, a dandelion. The decisions are made via adaptation, through genetic trial and error, taking thousands of generations and in some cases millions of years.

A huge number of species, including alligators, avocado trees, and tropical fish, made the "decision" long ago to not even bother with winter. My neighbor made the same decision last year and now winters in Miami. There certainly is some sense in this nonconfrontational approach. Most of the world's living things live in perpetual summer; relatively few are equipped for winter.

"Leaving" for the winter doesn't always mean not showing up in the first place; another way to "leave" is to simply die. This is the tried-and-true response of all our annual plants and several of our insects and spiders. This ultimate decrease in energy demands is not as draconian as it may sound. It is a successful strategy. The key is to leave behind some seeds or eggs, whatever the case may be, for next spring.

I think most of us would equate this concept of leaving for the winter with migration, a strategy seldom found in the plant kingdom for obvious reasons, but employed frequently by birds, the most mobile segment of the animal kingdom. Broad-winged hawks, for example, will mass in the tens of thousands for an energy-depleting, 3,000-mile flight from the cold. Some years, only half of the birds survive the round trip to the tropics and back to the North Woods. Migration takes its toll, but so does winter.

For the species that have evolved the capability of toughing it out, there are two options: activity and inactivity. Activity means work to make up for the sun's laziness. It's the mind-boggling metabolism of the chickadee that raises the temperature of its golf-ball-size body to 110 degrees. And it's the voracious appetite of the short-tailed shrew that won't allow it to stop its subnivean insect hunting for more than a matter of minutes, lest it keel over and die. And, for you and me, it's the harvesting of trees, the mining of oil and coal, and the preserving of food.

Inactivity, practiced by dormant perennial plants, is also employed by the couch potatoes of the animal and human world. Inactivity lowers energy needs. The white-tailed deer will do its best to fatten up in the fall in preparation to stand in one place and nibble on twigs all winter long. Honey bees will cram into the hive and beavers will huddle in the lodge, using each other for insulation. Bears, woodchucks, and chipmunks go beyond behavior modification; winter conditions trigger an internal metabolic shutdown in the stingiest balance of the energy budget – hibernation.

Cold-blooded creatures have the toughest row to hoe. Like our friend the woolly bear, or the turtles and salamanders burrowed into the mud, insects, reptiles, and amphibians have to find a winter home that will hopefully stay above freezing. Some garter snakes have been found frozen solid in midwinter – remarkably, a survivable predicament for them.

Winter storms help these critters by blanketing their subterranean beds with a life-saving insulation layer, often provided by a northeaster, or, recognizing the ol' New England fondness for contractions, a nor'easter. This fabled storm is fed by a giant counterclockwise swirl of energy whose northeast wind scoops moisture from the Atlantic, freezes it, and deposits it inland as warmth to the burrowing shrew, as joy to the soon-to-be-out-of-school child, and as a surprise to the meteorologist.

Winter transforms. But, to me, it does so in a manner that is non-threatening because winter is temporary. To winter is to survive, not to change. Winter is respite and it is renewal. Fighting it causes frustration, embracing it brings strength. For the woolly bear, the woodchuck, the spruce tree, the snow flea, and the meteorologist, winter is perfect. Every year, a familiar visit. Every year, a perfect beginning.

Dave Thurlow is the host, writer, and Executive Producer of The Weather Notebook, *a nationally syndicated radio program. He is employed by The Mount Washington Observatory where, besides producing a radio show, he has served as a weather observer, an educator, and is currently developing the Weather Discovery Center, to be opened in 1999 as the nation's first weather science center. His essays on weather have appeared in AMC* Outdoors *and* Weatherwise. *Dave and his wife Judy live in Jackson, New Hampshire.*

C. Ralph Adler

My father had two great love affairs in his life, and one was with his farm. He first laid eyes on those 100 acres of remote Rhode Island land, a weary apple orchard, in 1953 and since then he's done everything you can do to a piece of land: level it, plant seeds in it, put holes in it, extract twisted stumps out of it, pick rocks from it, clear trees off it. To Carl Adler, a great day is one in which he literally makes the earth move.

Dad called the farm Clear Acres, which speaks of the respect he has for order over sentiment. He believes that a man can reshape the world in his vision with bare hands and raw will. He saw, in his mind, his own Ponderosa and made it real. His allies in this mission were boys and machines. Alone at first, he was armed only with a second-hand GMC stake body truck and a Ford tractor. When he was done, he had eight sons and a full fleet of brightly painted trucks, tractors, bulldozers, and backhoes, all lined up, as he liked to say, "like tin soldiers."

The pursuit of this vision was driven more by passion than economics (Dad had a nine-to-five job, too). The costs were high. Thousands of days and nights of body-breaking labor. Many other life choices left unexplored. The strained favor of a tolerant wife. But these were all calculated choices. The line between want and need is often unclear, but Dad was motivated by both. He *had* to make clover thrive in once stony soil, whittle stands of trees into mountains of cord wood, and capture a pond in a spot where nature had not thought to put one.

Nothing, however, defines my father better than his 50-year battle with snow.

Fascinated by great steel machines, obsessed with being outside, and certain that in a hand-to-hand contest between humans and nature, humans can win, he took up plowing snow in 1947. He was 16. It was light work at first, plowing local bus routes and helping people out with their driveways. Five years later, married and just settled on the farm, he began the steady climb to bigger equipment and bigger jobs as an on-call contractor for the state of Rhode Island.

"Between the woods and frozen lake ... "

Dad paints a lonesome image of one man stepping into the fury of nor'easters, blizzards, and ice storms in those early days. "The first route they gave me was the Wallum Lake run," a desolate stretch in northwest Rhode Island that even today must look forsaken and lightless to pilots flying over at night. "It was about the toughest route you could get. It was hilly, and I had that little truck. I used to pray that it wouldn't quit because there were no other trucks with me. Everybody went to bed there at nine o' clock, so you wouldn't see a light 'til six in the morning."

He was one of a small but close group of men (I haven't yet met a woman snow plower) who took on this work. When the wet and the cold and the loneliness got to be too much, Dad would gather with other plowers at the Chepachet state garage, a tin shed that served as a Department of Transportation outpost. Friendships began there as the men stopped in for a little comfort and companionship. "There was a pot belly stove they'd heat with old guard rails and lumber the guys picked up. If you sat within ten feet of it, you'd melt. If you sat within twelve feet, it was comfortable. If you sat fourteen feet, you froze."

For the 50s, the money was good and probably helped justify leaving a warm bed. "When I first started with the state, I got $12 an hour. That was for the man, the truck, the plow. By today's standards that doesn't seem like an awful lot of money."

He eyes my mother, Barbara, fondly. "So we'd get a check from the state for two or three, or four hundred dollars, and Sweetie Pie and I thought we were rich."

For a while, the one-man operation was enough to help Dad break into the business and get his feet wet, so to speak. Year by year, he added more trucks and enlisted local buddies to give up their winter days and nights to keeping the roads clear. "George Leach drove, Billy Davis drove, Frankie Davis drove, Johnny Leach drove. But it was difficult because all these other fellas had other jobs, and if they don't get out of work 'til six and the state wants you at four … but we got through it all right."

Then the kids started coming. Mom gave birth eight times in eleven years, all boys. Most of them fell in behind Dad, heirs to his ideology as much as his bone structure. As early as Mom would allow it, the boys were helping in the garage. By ten or twelve, they were driving tractors or trucks on the farm. By legal driving age, and sometimes earlier (by necessity), they were on the road, full partners with Dad in his way of life, a band of warriors chasing adventure in the snow.

"… the darkest evening of the year."

Snow has no agenda. It has no emotion, no mission. A flake of snow begins as a speck of dust bobbing around high in the atmosphere. When it's cold enough and there's enough water in the air and water vapor condenses below the freezing point, ice crystals attach themselves to the particle interlocking into six-sided, symmetrical shapes. It's mechanical and (somewhat) predictable, a function of physics, not design. A gathering storm doesn't decide, "I'm gonna whack the heck out of New England today."

Yet humans take the forecast of snow as a call to arms, a challenge from an enemy in the sky. In other kinds of catastrophic weather – hurricanes, tornadoes, duststorms – the usual impulse is to hunker down and clean up later. But with snowstorms, the battle is joined with the storm in progress, and there is only one imperative: *keep the roads open.* Snow plowers are the front-liners in this defense of our right to move around as we please.

When Dad and my brothers sit around the dinner table to talk about the snow plowing days, the stories are about danger and strategies. Dad doesn't scare easily (although one of his more endearing qualities is that he falls apart at the sight of blood), but he has once or twice met his match with snow and its colder-hearted counterpart, ice. "Plowing snow is easy," he says. "It's the ice storms you really have no control over. You can't scrape the roads, you just have to treat them. As far as I'm concerned, the scariest night I remember was the time we had an ice storm. Kenny and Bruce were with me. They sent us up to 146, we had the B42. We came over the hill, and there were tanker trucks from Worcester all stopped with their blinker lights on. The road looked like a pond." My brother Kenny adds, "The trucks were all lined up on the side of the road … it looked like a runway," like planes waiting for takeoff.

"This was two or three o'clock in the morning, cold, and oh, raining...." Dad says. The misery of the memory causes him to stop and relive it for a moment. "We only had six yards of sand ... that's all we had," and the job ahead seemed impossible. In fact, it was. "I could just picture us going over the side of the road," he says. There was only one option, other than to sit and wait. Using their own sand to treat the road behind them as they went, Dad, Kenny, and Bruce backed up 15 miles (at about ten miles an hour) to get off the road to safety. "We *backed up* from there almost to the Mass line," he says, shaking his head.

Another fearsome storm packed 50-mile-per-hour winds and ten-degree-below-zero temperatures. "We had a situation where even the state guys wouldn't go out. The storm was actually over, we'd worked a long time, and they called us and asked us if we'd come back to help them. They asked us to go Route 295 all the way up to the Massachusetts line, which is a long way for a truck at 15 miles per hour. What happened was, the snow was blowing across the road. It might be bare one place but two feet of snow up there." Dad listened hard when the state rep warned him, "'If the truck quits, just push it to the side of the road. Don't leave the guys in the truck. Don't get separated,' he said. 'Stay together.' It was brutal."

"We could drive for ten miles and not push anything," Kenny adds, "then we'd get to a section and it would look like a tunnel. We'd back up, plow through, and two hours later it was filled in again."

As it does for many, the blizzard of 1978 holds near mythic power for the family. Dad begins the story: "I was downtown that morning and I said to Barbara, 'I think we're going to get a pretty good storm today.' Now there was nothing in the forecast about the blizzard. Matt Kulik, who was in charge of highway maintenance for the state of Rhode Island calls me, so we had coffee at Sadie's. And we come out at ten o'clock and it was snowing really big flakes, and Matt says 'I think we're going to get some snow,' and I said, 'yeah.'"

Dad went back to the shop and, trusting instinct, decided to close the store and head home. "I just made the ramp getting on 195," he says of the rapidly accumulating snow. "I get to 295 and 6 and I tell ya you couldn't see the hood ornament. I come in the house and the state's on the phone saying send me two sanders. I said this guy's crazy! Two sanders?! We got six inches of snow out there! So I said to the kids, no, we're not going to go, we'll just wait. And sure enough, fifteen minutes later they call and say send me all the plows."

Bruce (the third son, if you're keeping track) mostly remembers that storm because it got so bad, they had to "walk" a bulldozer from the farm to Route 295. The storm had begun to outmatch trucks and plows, and heavier equipment was called for. But the snow had become so deep a truck carrying a bulldozer could not make it through. At a snail's pace of four miles per hour, the boys drove the bulldozer to the interstate.

Kenny (second son) has a clear memory of a near collision with oblivion during the blizzard. "Gerry and I were going down a ramp off 295 and I swear to God,

I couldn't see where I was going. I stopped the truck and there was a mountain of snow in front of me that was about 30 feet high. I'm looking at this thing and all of a sudden Dad tapped on the door and asked, 'Where are you going?' I say I don't know, look at the drift." It was no drift. "It was a ledge," says Kenny, who had lost his way off the ramp in the deceiving whiteness and nearly hit a literal stone wall.

The storm became increasingly surreal as the intensity moved beyond anything the boys had experienced before. At one point Dad "hit a wall of snow and the truck just went boom, stopped. I got out and looked and it was up to the radiator. I couldn't go forward and I couldn't go backward because there were two trucks in back of me. I looked across the highway and there was Kenny coming down the other direction. He had to go up to another exit, come down 295 (the wrong way) and put a chain on me." Soon, though, it was time to give up the fight to keep the road open. "A state cop comes over, knocked on the door and says you got to forget about plowing. We got to get these people out of their cars! They were afraid people would die." Interstate 295 was like an ice age burial ground, with dozens of lumbering vehicles stuck with their occupants still inside them.

"They were stranded. The cops said just take them anywhere so they can get inside," Dad recalls. "And now we're losing the road ... "

At this point in the story, Ken takes issue with Dad's pronouncement of failure. "We didn't lose the road. We kept it open." Mom chimes in: "Scotty lost the road, though." (Scott is son number five.) "We came to the Centredale exit and he was parked there and came up beside me and Dad and said, 'Can't make it ... can't go through.' And Dad said, 'Get out of the way. I'll go through.' And he did."

The blizzard, which Kenny describes as "a hurricane but in the wintertime," kept the crew out for 48 hours straight with no sleep. "I told the state the guys are dead tired, we're going to kill someone. They said, all right, go home for eight hours then come back." But while coming back resulted in an eight-foot wide tunnel that did keep the interstate passable (Dad boasts that their stretch of road stayed open, but it took the Army to open the rest of it), extra duty was required. "After the storm was over," Kenny says, "we had a state cop with us and he says we have to go find all the cars and make sure nobody's in 'em. I don't think I went 100 yards down the road, I had the wing plow, and I took the roof right off a car. The cop gets out, he looks inside, and says, 'nobody in this one.'"

Dad had a similar experience: "I'm about four feet off the ground pushing the snow back and I heard the crunch ... I went into the back end of a car, took the front door, right through the windshield. There was a state cop in back of me and I said, 'Jeez, I tuned that one up pretty good, didn't I?' And he says, 'This is an emergency! Keep going!' Never heard a word about it."

One state trooper was almost not so lucky. Kenny was pushing his way up the highway where a trooper was on the side of the road, stuck. But Kenny couldn't see him in all the snow. "He saw me comin', he said all he could see was snow going like this [shooting up in the air] both ways," Kenny recalls. "He got out of the car and ran. I couldn't stop in time and I buried his car. Blew out the rear window, the side window, and the windshield. He comes over, laughin' his butt off, and says, 'You shoulda seen what this thing looked like!' That's the damage, and the power."

When the storm had ended, and the work was done, the Adler crew headed home, but even that was not easy. "I don't know how many days we were out there, I lost track," says Kenny. "We came home one night, nobody's out, everything's stopped, and we got to the corner of the driveway [a half-mile from home] and the drive shaft blew on the V plow. So we had to walk in." With most familiar landmarks smothered by the thick blanket of snow, and no moon, they followed the stone wall at the farm's edge to get them back home.

"But I have promises to keep ... "

As with any group of humans who converge to achieve a task or accomplish a goal, snow plowing has a kind of culture, and there are rules. The first rule of snow plowing is, *nothing is more important than the storm.*

I learned this one night when Dad must have had trouble scaring up enough guys to help him. He asked me to come out and give him a hand. He had figured out a long time ago that this kind of work was not my thing, that I was the one son who had chosen a different path. But he must have been desperate. It was a brutal storm, a cold, sloppy stew of ice shards, sleet, and snow driven by a screeching wind. The kind of storm you can barely stand up in.

Luck was not with Dad that night. The trucks' engines were fussy. He ran from one truck to the other trying to make them work, like a mad scientist pulling levers and pushing buttons. He hurled curses at them as if he could bully them into turning over. The sky and my father were shrieking at each other. I looked up and actually felt like someone was knuckle-balling chunks of ice at me, as if Thor and a couple of his buddies were on a real bender and this was how they were getting their kicks.

Dad gave me a can of ether to spray somewhere into one of the engines while he worked the key and pumped the gas, cursing all the way. I suspected from the smell that this was flammable stuff, and I suddenly felt my death was near; the question was would it be death by ice (from the sky) or fire (from an exploding aerosol can)? I extended my arm toward the engine, Dad's patience thinning to near cataclysm, my finger poised over the nozzle. I turned my head, closed my eyes hard, and fired. The engine coughed and spat. "Again!" Dad yelled and, again, I pressed the nozzle. With a guttural expulsion of smoke, the truck awoke, snarling into service. For Dad, that was one small victory in a night full of battles. For me, it sealed my personal philosophy about what to do in a winter storm: *let it snow.*

While I could not embrace their at-all-costs conviction, Dad and the boys would give up almost anything to keep plowing. Comfort, food, sleep. "You leave here and you never know when you're coming back," Dad says. "We didn't know if we'd be gone twelve hours or thirty hours. Sometimes I'd work downtown eight hours, come home at six, then go plowing all that night and the next day. You'd come home when you're done."

Plowing snow is about endurance, moving down a tunnel with no light at the end. It's lonesome. Even when you're with someone, it's hard to make conversation last three days. It's either too cold (drafty truck cabs with the wind blowing around your legs) or too hot (Dad says nobody wanted to drive with him, because he cranked the heat to 85 or 90 degrees; enough, he says, to melt the rubber on the windshield wipers sometimes). Food doesn't last long; although Mom would pack lots of sandwiches, they would be gone in hours, and in a snowstorm, restaurants don't stay open for business.

Then there's the hypnotic effect of the snow coming at you, directly at your face and falling away on all sides like an endless passing field of stars. "When you're drivin' you couldn't look at the snow goin' into the lights, it would put you right to sleep," says Chris (the youngest son). "You had to look over the side, or up. If the road was any type of bare at all, you could follow the windrow (the row of snow pushed back by the plow) with your peripheral vision, but if you stared straight ..." The boys also say one rule of the road was to turn off your blinking lights if you were in a convoy, because the driver behind you could be mesmerized, and lulled to sleep, by the constant blink ... blink ... blink ...

"I'd say the toughest thing was fightin' to stay awake," says Scott, "stickin' your head out the window." Dad learned that the worst time to fight the fatigue was "when the sun is comin' up in the morning, say 6 o'clock. The minute the sun comes up, you're fightin' it. When the sun comes up after an hour or so, you get a shot of energy. Night and day is easy."

For the women in the lives of these men, snow plowing was an initiation into the family, a good way of finding out who these guys really are, and a study of a kind of obsession. Taking your girlfriend with you snow plowing was kind of cool. For awhile. Donna, Scott's wife, tells of what she calls the "30-hour storm," which set her against snow plowing for life. "I don't remember stopping for a bathroom or food. It wasn't fun. For a couple of hours it's fun, but after a long time you can't stop ... it made me very upset. I wanted to go home, and he said, 'I can't take you home.'" Mom jumps into the story: "I think you were pregnant, weren't you? I remember being in the other truck and thinking, oh, my God ... " Debbie, Bruce's wife, remembers wishing the trucks would break down so everyone would *have* to go home.

Lynda, Kenny's wife, had a similar experience but had a few strings to pull to get home. "It was bad when they say I'm going out for an hour, and they end up staying two days," she says. "She was with me on 295," Kenny says. "I told her we're not gonna be long, it's a short storm, but it was goin' on the second day. There was a statie right on the overpass, and I say, 'Hey, you have to get my girlfriend home.' He says, 'Oh, yeah, right.' And I say, 'It's Jack Devine's daughter.'" Jack Devine was a Captain in the State Police. "So he made a u-turn and said, 'I'll get her right home.'"

Snowstorms seemed to have a nasty habit of coming on special days. "We worked Thanksgiving, we worked Christmas, we worked New Year's. We even plowed snow on Easter Sunday," Dad says. "Is that the day it melted in the afternoon? It went up to 65 degrees," Bruce remembers. "We went like a bastard to get it plowed before the snow melted," Kenny says with a laugh. "Yeah, the guy from the state said you better hurry before this stuff melts!" Chris remembers one Christmas night when he "sat there all night on a holiday night" in a backhoe at a sandpile, waiting to fill up sanders. "I think I only filled four trucks, all night, and I thought this is the most stupid thing. I'm 16 years old, what am I doing here?"

The "never stop" philosophy prevailed even over inevitable sleep. Mike (son number four) was known to the others as "the snoozemaster" because he had a habit of falling asleep at the wheel. "We were always beepin' the horn at him, come on Mike, wake up!" Chris says. One day Mike was teaching Chris how to drive while plowing. Chris was 15. "Mike was drivin' in the middle of the night; we used to go slow, maybe eighteen miles an hour, so that doesn't take much. But he's drivin' and fallin' asleep and the truck was pretty much just goin'. I'm awake, goin' oh my God, he's fallin' asleep. So every time he'd fall behind, I'd reach over with my left foot and hit the gas and grab the steerin' wheel. He got wind that I was doin' it, so I'm steerin' the truck and hittin' the gas pedal with my foot and he's asleep. We'd get to the turnaround and, whoop, 'Mike, wake up!' He'd turn around, then the same thing ... he falls back asleep, my left foot's on the gas, and I'm steerin'."

Once Kenny was riding with a hired driver at age 14. Turns out the driver couldn't handle the truck after having a little to drink before the trip, so Kenny took over. "He couldn't shift, couldn't drive, so after about the fifth try I say, 'Hey, you want me to get it up the hill for you?'" Kenny says. "I got it up the hill, and I kept goin'. A couple of hours later, something happened to the carburetor, and the only way we could get it to work is he had to get out on the fender and play with the choke. I'm drivin' the truck, he's on the fender, we're plowin' snow. 'Hey, how you doin' out there?' I would yell. 'Oh, it's nice and warm in here near the engine, you know,' he said."

A second major rule of the snow plowing culture is *be nice, but not too nice.* The snow isn't the only menace; sometimes storms bring out the worst in people, too. Years ago, "people driving would stay behind you because they knew the road was plowed," Kenny recalls. "Then, when you got past their exit, they got off and sometimes they'd blink their lights to say thanks. As time went on, they just wanted to get out in front of you, so we let 'em go. A lot of times they'd go 100 yards and do a couple of 360's, and go off the road."

Chris adds that trouble can start when "you start being a nice guy, you start helping people. If you pull up on somebody and they're in a ditch that's one thing, but if they fly by you on the wrong side, you don't help them." Dad continues that getting out to help someone in a storm can buy you misery for the rest of the trip: "You stop to help somebody and you're nice and dry, and you gotta get a chain, and put the chain under the back or whatever. Now you're gettin' wet, they're just sittin' in the car, not helpin'."

"The minute they say don't bend my bumper," Kenny adds, "that's when you take the chain away. They look at you and say, 'Hey, where are you goin',' and you say, 'I'm sorry, I can't touch your car.'"

Sometimes the tricky parts come when someone else is just trying to have fun. "We did the milk run, on Cherry Hill Road," Kenny says, "and one day Mr. Leach was drivin' and this thing jumps out in front of the plow. It was a kid. They get thrills from jumpin' in front of the plow and havin' the plow throw them off. We came back the next time and the same kid nailed me in the side of the head with a snowball. The two of us got out and tried to chase him. We made snowballs and kept them in the truck, and went lookin' for that kid."

"... and miles to go before I sleep."

Plowing snow took its toll on the family. My mother was willing to put up with almost anything in my Dad's quests, but her nerves could grow thin. Like the time she looked out the window, up the long driveway, to see a 10-ton truck sliding *sideways* down the hill on a sheet of ice. "That was scary," she says. "I was waiting for the guys to come home, I knew they'd be home soon, and I looked up and there's headlights going across the field, over to the stone wall. I thought, what fool is up there ... the truck is coming down sideways!" Or the time when Bruce's finger was nearly cut in half when a plow was dropped on it. Or the time, alone at home with three young children, crisis struck.

"That was the worst storm I ever remember," Mom says. "It was really windy, whistling through all the windows. We had bad windows in those days, and the curtains were out straight." Something had gone wrong with the furnace. "Every radiator in the house was blowing steam, the windows were saturated, the walls were saturated. I didn't know what to do. I woke up in the morning and the kids said, 'Mommy, there's snow on the window, you can't see out the window.'" She was forced to turn off the heat, and live by the fireplace for two days. Stories like that aside, Mom simply remembers all the waiting. Looking out the living room window for the trucks to come over the hill.

After many years of surrendering their lives to the weather, one by one the members of the family realized that the snow plowing days had to come to an end. "There's a limit to everything," says Donna. "What bothered me most is all the hours they worked, then Scott would come home and didn't have enough time to go out and play with the kids in the snow. I dreaded snow because their association was when it snowed, dad wouldn't be home and the kids wouldn't have fun. So winter was a bad time, because we lost family time. I had great memories growing up of being with my parents in the snow, but my kids will remember him coming home and being totally exhausted."

"There was a time it was worth it," Kenny says, especially when you bought a $100,000 truck and had to get your money's worth out of it. "But it got to the point where we looked at snow plowing and called it blood money. Slowly but surely, we took one truck off, then another truck off." Dad, the first to get out on the road, was the last to let go. "The boys gave it up and I kept it up for a couple of years."

"He thought we were nuts," Kenny says.

One reason the boys decided to quit, said Kenny, is "I don't think people appreciate it. They think you're plowin' in their driveways, the pay raise hasn't gone up in five years, and they think you're makin' a lot of money." Chris adds, "People don't care that you worked all night in the roads. They get up in the morning to go to work, you're goin' slow, in their way, they're beepin' their horns and givin' you a gesture. What's that all about?"

But most of it was just plain getting weary of the grind. Dad says now, "You'd drive by a guy's house, and he's got the TV on, and the fireplace is goin', and you're in a damn bumpy truck and sayin' what the hell am I doin' in this thing?"

A residual effect of the experience is a sense of having learned something, of gaining more than a layman's understanding of the weather. "Every storm has its own personality," says Kenny. "You can get a nice fluffy storm, and it's a joy. You get out of the truck, the snow falls off you. You get a wet storm, it takes forever to dry and you're miserable. Sometimes you leave here and it's a joy to be plowing, other times you look at the road and you don't want to be there. You get to know what it's going to be like. Some storms, it's like a flu. It doesn't want to quit."

There's relief in the family now that a crew of eight or ten doesn't have to scramble to ready its fleet of trucks and plows every time there's a forecast of snow, although Dad can still be seen moving from window to window, looking for the first flakes of a new storm. He still gets up at five in the morning to plow his driveway. For my brothers, the years of fighting snow have left different lasting impressions. Kenny still loves a good snowfall, going for rides in it, predicting what kind of storm it will be by how wet or fine the flakes are. But Mike says, "I don't miss it at all. It scarred me. I don't like the snow. I used to love it, but not any more. I think it's just a nuisance."

For most, there's just the final reward of being in a nice warm bed when the snow is falling outside. "It's nice," Chris says, "when you come out of work, especially on a Saturday afternoon, and it's snowin' and you can look up and say, jeez, I'm goin' home."

C. Ralph Adler lives in Brentwood, New Hampshire with his wife, Dani, and daughters Bryn and Caleigh. A writer, editor, and filmmaker, he is a Senior Research Associate at RMC Research Corporation, providing consulting, evaluation, and product development in the fields of educational media, children's television, informal science education, school improvement, and family literacy. A former news editor for The New Hampshire Times, *he writes essays, fiction, and poetry.*

JOIN THE OBSERVATORY

MOUNT WASHINGTON offers a perspective on weather and the mountain environment unlike any other. Since 1932, the Mount Washington Observatory staff has monitored the elements from a vantage point atop this 6288-foot peak, the highest in the Northeast. Today, while the staff continues to provide regional atmospheric information to the National Weather Service and record weather observations, the scope of the Observatory has broadened to encompass a wide range of exciting research projects and educational programs both on and off the mountain.

The highest wind-speed ever recorded – 231 mph – was clocked by Observatory staff on April 12, 1934.

You'll have a whole new view on the weather, history, and the White Mountains when you become a member of the Mount Washington Observatory.

Visit the highest museum in the Northeast – the Mount Washington Museum – with its exhibits on the mountain's geology, meteorology, zoology, botany and history. There's also a new Weather Discovery Room with interactive exhibits and experiments, encouraging you to participate in the basics of weather observation. Members can take part in unique winter overnight workshops on the summit, too.

Above treeline, vegetation is tough enough to stand some of the world's worst weather, but so fragile visitors must tread carefully. Here, much can be learned about the effects of extreme weather conditions.

For a wide selection of books, weather instruments, educational toys and White Mountain artwork, members can visit the Museum Shop in two locations: on the summit, and in the new Weather Discovery Center in North Conway, New Hampshire. Members get a 10% discount.

The Observatory also comes to you right where you live: you can hear *The Weather Notebook* – the Observatory's acclaimed syndicated radio program – on over 250 public and commercial stations nationwide, and internationally on *Voice of America*.

In 1999, the Observatory opened the Weather Discovery Center in North Conway village – a year 'round facility devoted entirely to weather, it is one of the first of its kind to be built anywhere in the world. The Center has interactive displays and games describing wind, snow and storms; an audio-visual theater with exciting multimedia presentations; a re-creation of the 1934 Observatory building, where the World Record Wind of 231 mph was recorded; and the latest in forecasting computer modeling and technology from the National Oceanic and Atmospheric Administration (NOAA). There is also a live video feed from the summit observatory. The Center was established with support from NOAA, the National Science Foundation, and Observatory members.

Too far away to visit the Observatory in person? Join us at www.mountwashington.org and find out the current conditions on the summit. Or take a look at the view through the live camera from the Observatory's windows. Play a weather game or two, read up on some history, and visit the gallery of beautiful Mount Washington photographs.

The Observatory has facilities atop Mount Washington and on Route 16 in North Conway, New Hampshire (at the northern end of the village). Contact us at P. O. Box 2310, North Conway, NH 03860-2310. Telephone 603-356-2137. Fax 603-356-0307. questions@mountwashington.org.

The Observatory and Museum atop Mount Washington are open from mid-May to mid-October, (weather permitting).

Members can volunteer to live and work at the summit throughout the year.

Members' contributions help support the Observatory's activities in wind, ice and fog research. Airplane icing is just one area currently being researched.

MEMBERSHIP BENEFITS

- A subscription to *Windswept,* the Observatory's quarterly magazine
- Free admission to the Summit Museum and the Weather Discovery Center
- A 10% discount on Museum Shop purchases
- Access to Observatory tours, EduTrips, Sunrise on the Summit programs, and unique volunteer opportunities
- Access to the Observatory's extensive archive of historical books, maps and photographs in the Gladys Brooks Memorial Library

PRODUCTION NOTES

Paul Breeden created his black-and-white illustrations with a variety of materials, including paper, scratchboard, calfskin and sheepskin vellum (the traditional book pages used by the mediaeval scribes), and pen-and-ink. Paul painted the cover image with hand-made, natural minerals, earth colors, and organic pigment paints. The deep-blue sky is touched with the brilliance of pure lapis lazuli (as mentioned in Paul's essay). Other colors, including the azurite blue, were obtained from Hopi Indian and Australian Aboriginal sources and were then formulated into workable watercolor paints.

Soul of the Sky was designed and typeset within view of Mount Washington by Bruce Kennett and Dodie Coman, who are delighted to live, work and play amid the skies of the White Mountains. The book was composed in Giovanni Mardersteig's "Dante" types, using Monotype's digital version of the original hot-metal designs. Dante is classified as an old-style type, but it has somewhat darker "color" than many old-styles, and a particularly pleasing italic. Dante was developed in the early 1950s by Mardersteig and French punch-cutter Charles Malin, as a private type for use in Mardersteig's own book-printing companies in Italy. The type was first used in Mardersteig's 1955 edition of Boccaccio's *Trattatello in laude di Dante*, and takes its name from it. Once Dante was made available as a commercial font through the English Monotype Company, it was eagerly adopted by book printers everywhere.

Thomson-Shore, Inc. printed and bound the book, using vegetable-based inks and a special text paper milled by Glatfelter – recycled, acid-free, and free of elemental chlorine. The binding is Smyth-sewn in traditional signatures, not merely glued. This means that the book you are holding will have a long life, its pages will not become brittle or fall out, and it will open easily for more pleasurable reading.